# OPERALIA

Books LLC®, Reference Series, Memphis, USA, 2011. www.booksllc.net. Copyright: http://creativecommons.org/licenses/by-sa/3.0/deed.en

## Table of Contents

**Operalia**
Operalia, The World Opera Competition ................................................. 1
Plácido Domingo ............................... 2

**Operalia prize-winners**
Ainhoa Arteta ...................................... 6
Alexey Kudrya ..................................... 6
Ana María Martínez ............................ 7
Andión Fernández ............................... 9
Angel Blue .......................................... 9
Arturo Chacón Cruz .......................... 10

Brian Asawa ...................................... 11
Carlos Cosías .................................... 11
David Bižić ........................................ 12
Elizabeth Futral ................................. 13
Eric Owens (bass-baritone) .............. 13
Erwin Schrott .................................... 14
Giuseppe Filianoti ............................. 15
Inva Mula .......................................... 15
Isabel Bayrakdarian ........................... 16
Joseph Calleja ................................... 17
Joseph Kaiser .................................... 18
José Cura .......................................... 18

Joyce DiDonato ................................. 19
Kate Aldrich ...................................... 21
Lisette Oropesa ................................. 22
Maria Fontosh .................................. 22
Mikhail Petrenko ............................... 23
Nina Stemme ..................................... 23
Robert Pomakov ............................... 24
Rolando Villazón .............................. 24
Susanna Phillips ................................. 25
Thiago Arancam ................................ 26

## Introduction

Purchase of this book entitles you to a free trial membership in the publisher's book club at www.booksllc.net. (Time limited offer.) Simply enter the barcode number from the back cover onto the membership form. The book club entitles you to select from hundreds of thousands of books at no additional charge. You can also download a digital copy of this and related books to read on the go. Simply enter the title or subject onto the search form to find them.

Each chapter in this book ends with a URL to a hyperlinked online version. Type the URL exactly as it appears. If you change the URL's capitalization it won't work. Use the online version to access related pages, websites, footnotes, tables, color photos, updates. Click the version history tab to see the chapter's contributors. Click the edit link to suggest changes.

A large and diverse editor base collaboratively wrote the book, not a single author. After a long process of discussion and debate, the chapters gradually took on a neutral point of view reached through consensus. Additional editors expanded and contributed to chapters striving to achieve balance and comprehensive coverage. This reduced the regional or cultural bias found in many other books and provided access and breadth on subject matter otherwise little documented.

## Operalia, The World Opera Competition

**Operalia, The World Opera Competition** is an annual international competition for young opera singers. Founded in 1993 by renowned tenor Plácido Domingo, the competition has helped launch the careers of several important artists, such as Brian Asawa, José Cura, Joyce DiDonato, Elizabeth Futral, Inva Mula and Ana María Martínez.

### Overview

Operalia is based in Paris, France but hosts its competition in a different city each year. Cities which have hosted the competition include Paris at both the Palais Garnier and Théâtre du Châtelet, Mexico City at the Televisa Recording Studios, Madrid at the Teatro de la Zarzuela, Bordeaux at the Grand Théâtre, Tokyo at the Kan-I Hoken Hall, Hamburg at the Hamburg Music Hall, Puerto Rico at the Luis A. Ferré Performing Arts Center, Los Angeles at both UCLA's Royce Hall and the Dorothy Chandler Pavilion, Washington, D.C. at George Washington University's Lisner Auditorium, the Lake Constance region in Austria, Germany and Switzerland, Madrid at the Teatro Real, Valencia at the Palau de les Arts Reina Sofía, and Québec at the Palais Montcalm and Grand Théâtre de Québec.

The competition is open to singers between the ages of 18 and 30 who are already performing at a highly skilled level. All voice types of both sexes are able to compete. Participants in the competition are selected by audition through a submitted recording to Operalia. A panel of three judges listens and evaluates the audition tapes. Only the top 40 submissions are invited to compete in the competition. Typically the organization receives 800 to 1,000 submissions each year, making entry into the competition alone an honor.

The competition is presided over every year by Plácido Domingo, although he himself does not judge the competition. A jury of 10 opera directors from important opera houses all over the world is assembled to judge the competition. Competitors must prepare 4 arias for the competition which consists of four rounds. In the first round each singer gets to choose one aria they want to sing and then the jury selects the other aria from their list of four for them to perform. Singers can also compete in a separate zarzuela competition. If they choose to do so they would perform an additional zarzuela piece in each round.

Of the 40 singers, half of them are eliminated in the first round. The second round involves the performance of one more aria, after which only 10 singers move on to the next round. Likewise, the third round eliminates half of the singers, leaving only five participants in the final round. The first three rounds are performed with piano accompaniment and the final round is sung with a symphonic orchestra conducted by Plácido Domingo.

Although only five singers make it into the final round, the competition has a total of 10 prizes which total up to 175,000 US dollars. In the general competition 1st prize, 2nd prize, and 3rd prize are awarded, one of each to both sexes, making a total of 6 prizes. Within the zarazuela competition two prizes are awarded, one to a male singer and one to a female singer. There is also a prize awarded by the audience of the final competition to one female singer and one male singer. It is possible for a singer to win more than one award. More important than the money received by the prize is the recognition and career boost given by the competition. It is normal for the opera directors judging the competition to engage competition winners for future opera performances with their companies, or for them to connect artists with other opera directors.

### Official website
- Official Website of Operalia, The World Opera Competition

Source (edited): "http://en.wikipedia.org/wiki/Operalia,_The_World_Opera_Competition"

# Plácido Domingo

Domingo speaks at the National Endowment for the Arts Opera Honors on October 31, 2008 in Washington, DC.

**José Plácido Domingo Embil** KBE (born 21 January 1941, Madrid), better known as **Plácido Domingo**, is a Spanish tenor and conductor known for his versatile and strong voice, possessing a ringing and dramatic tone throughout its range. In March 2008, he debuted in his 128th opera role, giving Domingo more roles than any other tenor. One of The Three Tenors, he has also taken on conducting opera and concert performances, as well as serving as the General Director of the Washington National Opera in Washington, D.C. and the Los Angeles Opera in California. His contract in Los Angeles has been extended through the 2012-13 season, but the Washington, D.C. will end with the 2010–2011 season.

## Biography and career

### Early years

Plácido Domingo (1979)

Plácido Domingo was born on January 21, 1941, near the Barrio de Salamanca section of Madrid, Spain, and moved to Mexico with his family, who ran a zarzuela company. He studied piano at first privately and later at the National Conservatory of Music in Mexico City.

In 1957, P. Domingo made his first professional appearance, performing with his mother in a concert at Mérida, Yucatán. He made his opera debut performing in Manuel Fernández Caballero's zarzuela, *Gigantes y cabezudos*, singing a baritone role. At that time, he was working with his parents' zarzuela company, taking baritone roles and as an accompanist for other singers. Among his first performances was a minor role in the first Mexican production of *My Fair Lady* where he was also the assistant conductor and assistant coach. The company gave 185 performances, which included a production of Lehár's *The Merry Widow* in which he performed alternately as either Camille or Danilo.

In 1959, Domingo auditioned for the Mexico National Opera as a baritone but was then asked to sight-read some arias and lines in the tenor range. Finally he was accepted in the National Opera as a tenor comprimario and as a tutor for other singers. He provided backup vocals for *Los Black Jeans* in 1958, a rock-and-roll band led by César Costa. He studied piano and conducting, but made his stage debut acting in a minor role in 1959 (12 May) at the Teatro Degollado in Guadalajara as Pascual in *Marina*. It was followed by Borsa in *Rigoletto* (with Cornell MacNeil and Norman Treigle also in the cast), Padre Confessor (*Dialogues of the Carmelites*) and others.

He played piano for a ballet company to supplement his income as well as playing piano for a program on Mexico's newly founded cultural television station. The program consisted of excerpts from zarzuelas, operettas, operas, and musical comedies. He acted in a few small parts while at the theater in plays by Federico García Lorca, Luigi Pirandello, and Anton Chekhov.

**1960s–1980s**

In 1961, he made his operatic debut in a leading role as Alfredo in *La Traviata* at Monterrey (Maria Teresa Montoya theater) and, later in the same year, his debut in the United States with the Dallas Civic Opera, where he played the role of Arturo in Donizetti's *Lucia di Lammermoor* opposite Joan Sutherland in the title role.

In 1962, he returned to Texas to play the role of Edgardo in the same opera with Lily Pons at the Fort Worth Opera. At the end of 1962, he signed a six month contract with the Israel National Opera in Tel Aviv but later extended the contract and stayed for two and a half years, singing 280 performances of 12 different roles.

In June 1965, after finishing his contract with Israel National Opera, Domingo went for an audition at the New York City Opera and scheduled to make his New York debut as Don Jose in Bizet's *Carmen* but his debut came earlier when he was asked to fill in for an ailing tenor at the last minute in Puccini's *Madama Butterfly*. On 17 June 1965, Domingo made his New York debut as B. F. Pinkerton at the New York City Opera. In February 1966, he sang the title role in the U.S. premiere of Ginastera's *Don Rodrigo* at the New York City Opera, with much acclaim. The performance also marked the opening of the City Opera's new home at Lincoln Center.

His official debut at the Metropolitan Opera in New York occurred on 28 September 1968 when he substituted for Franco Corelli, in Cilea's *Adriana Lecouvreur* singing with Renata Tebaldi. Before *Adriana Lecouvreur*, he had sung in performances by the Metropolitan Opera at Lewisohn Stadium of Mascagni's *Cavalleria rusticana* and Leoncavallo's *Pagliacci* in 1966. Since then, he has opened the season at the Metropolitan Opera 21 times, surpassing the previous record of Enrico Caruso by four. He made his debut at the Vienna State Opera in 1967, at the Lyric Opera of Chicago in 1968, at both La Scala and San Francisco Opera in 1969, at the Philadelphia Lyric Opera Company in 1970, and at Covent Garden in 1971, and has now sung at practically every other important opera house and festival worldwide. In 1971, he sang Mario Cavaradossi in Puccini's *Tosca* at the Metropolitan Opera, and continued to sing that part for many years, singing it, in fact, more than any other role.

Domingo has also conducted opera–as early as 7 October 1973, *La traviata* at the New York City Opera with Patricia Brooks–and occasionally symphony orchestras as well. In 1981 Domingo gained considerable recognition outside of the opera world when he recorded the song "Perhaps Love" as a duet with the late American country/folk music singer John Denver. In 1987, he and Denver joined Julie Andrews for an Emmy Award winning holiday television special, *The Sound of Christmas*, filmed in Salzburg, Austria.

On 19 September 1985, the biggest earthquake in Mexico's history devastated part of the Mexican capital. Domingo's aunt, uncle, his nephew and his nephew's young son were killed in the collapse of the Nuevo León apartment block in the Tlatelolco housing complex. Domingo himself labored to rescue survivors. During the next year, he did benefit concerts for the victims and released an album of one of the events.

**1990s – present**

A statue in Mexico City as a recognition to his contributions to 1985 Mexico City earthquake victims and his artistic works

Throughout the 1990s and 2000s until today, Domingo continued performing, singing many of the same roles but adding new roles as well, among them the title roles in Wagner's *Parsifal* and Mozart's *Idomeneo*, Rossini's *Il barbiere di Siviglia* as Figaro, Wagner's *Die Walküre* as Siegmund, Lehár's *The Merry Widow* as Danilo and Alfano's *Cyrano de Bergerac* as Cyrano. From the middle 1990s to early in 2008 alone, he added 38 new roles to his repertoire, covering opera in six different languages (English, Italian, French, German, Russian and Spanish). The latest was the Italian opera by George Frideric Handel, *Tamerlano*.

Giving him even greater international recognition outside of the world of opera, he participated in The Three Tenors concert at the eve of the 1990 FIFA World Cup Final in Rome with José Carreras and Luciano Pavarotti. The event was originally conceived to raise money for the José Carreras International Leukemia Foundation and was later repeated a number of times, including at the three subsequent World Cup finals (1994 in Los Angeles, 1998 in Paris, and 2002 in Yokohama).

Alone, Domingo again made an appearance at the final of the 2006 World Cup in Berlin, along with rising stars Anna Netrebko and Rolando Villazón. On 24 August 2008, Domingo performed a duet with Song Zuying, singing *Ài de Huǒyàn (The Flame of Love)* at the 2008 Summer Olympics closing ceremony in Beijing. The Beijing Olympics was the second Olympics he performed at; he sang the Olympic Hymn at the closing ceremonies of the Barcelona Olympics. At the Olympic games that followed that, he would meet Sissel Kyrkjebø, who performed the Olympic Hymn at both the opening and closing ceremonies at those games.

In what has been called his 'final career move', Plácido Domingo announced on 25 January 2007 that in 2009 he would take on one of Verdi's most demanding baritone roles, singing the title role in *Simon Boccanegra*. The debut performance was at Berlin State Opera on October 24, followed by 29 other performances during 2009/2010 at major opera houses around the world. He would, however, continue to sing tenor roles beforehand and afterwards.

On 16–17 April 2008 he sang during the visit of Pope Benedict XVI at Nationals Park and at the Italian embassy in Washington D.C. Since 1990 Plácido Domingo has received many awards and honors for his achievement in the field of music and in recognition of his many benefit concerts and contributions to various charities.

On 15 March 2009, The Metropolitan Opera paid tribute to Domingo's 40th anniversary with the company with an on-stage gala dinner at the Met's 125th anniversary, commemorating his debut in Adriana Lecouvreur as Maurizio opposite Renata Tebaldi on 28 September 1968.

On 29 August 2009 he sang *Panis Angelicus* at the funeral mass of Senator Ted Kennedy in the Basilica of Our Lady of Perpetual Help in Boston, Massachusetts.

On September 20, 2010, Domingo announced that he would renew his contract as General Director of the Los Angeles Opera through 2013. On September 27, 2010, Domingo announced that he will not renew his contract as General Director of the Washington National Opera beyond its June 2011 expiration date.

Ever a sympathetic colleague, in March 2011 he refused to sing in Buenos Aires until the city settled a bitter musicians strike at the Teatro Colon .

## Family

He was born to Plácido Francisco Domingo Ferrer (8 March 1907 – 22 November 1987) and Pepita Embil Echaníz (28 February 1918 – 28 September 1994), two Spanish zarzuela stars who nurtured his early musical abilities. Domingo's father was half Catalan and half Aragonese while his mother was a Basque. His father was a violinist performing for opera and zarzuela orchestra. He was a baritone and actively taking roles in zarzuela. However his promising career as a baritone ended after he damaged his voice by singing with a cold. Domingo's mother was an established singer who made her zarzuela debut at the Gran Teatre del Liceu in Barcelona. She met her husband at age 21 while performing in Federico Moreno Torroba's *Sor Navarra*. In 1946 Moreno Torroba and Domingo's parents formed a zarzuela company and travelled frequently to Mexico. His parents later stayed permanently in Mexico and established their own zarzuela troupe, the Domingo-Embil Company. In addition to their son, they also have a daughter, Maria José Domingo de Fernandez .

On 29 August 1957 at age 16, Plácido Domingo married a fellow piano student, Ana María Guerra Cué (1938–2006) and his first son, José Plácido Domingo Guerra (Pepe) was born on 16 June 1958. However, the marriage didn't last long, the couple separating shortly thereafter. On 1 August 1962, Plácido Domingo married Marta Ornelas, born 1935, a lyric soprano from Veracruz, Mexico, whom he met during his conservatory days. In the same year, Marta had been voted "Mexican Singer of the Year" but she gave up her promising career to devote her time to her family. They have two sons, Plácido Francisco (Plácido Jr.) born on 21 October 1965 and Alvaro Maurizio born on 11 October 1968. After a period of time living in Israel, he and his family resided in Teaneck, New Jersey. During vacations, he usually spends his time with family in their vacation home in Acapulco, Mexico.

In March 2010 he underwent surgery for colon cancer.

## Recordings

He has made well over 100 recordings, most of which are full-length operas, often recording the same role more than once. Among these recordings is a boxed set of every tenor aria Verdi ever wrote, including several rarely performed versions, in different languages from the original operas, which Verdi wrote for specific performances.

In August 2005, EMI Classics released a new studio recording of Richard Wagner's *Tristan und Isolde* in which Domingo sings the title role of Tristan. A review of this recording, headlined "Vocal perfections", that appeared in the 8 August 2005 issue of *The Economist* begins with the word "Monumental" and ends with the words, "a musical lyricism and a sexual passion that make the cost and the effort entirely worthwhile". It characterized his July 2005 performance of Siegmund in Wagner's *Die Walküre* at Covent Garden as "unforgettable" and "luminous". The review also remarks that Domingo is still taking on roles that he has not previously performed.

Recordings that were released in 2006 include studio recordings of Puccini's *Edgar*, Isaac Albéniz's *Pepita Jiménez*, as well as a selection of Italian and Neapolitan songs, titled *Italia ti amo* (all three with Deutsche Grammophon). Domingo appeared as the star act in the New Orleans Opera Association's *A Night For New Orleans* with Frederica von Stade and Elizabeth Futral, in March 2006. The concert was to raise funds for the rebuilding of the city.

## Appearances on film and television

*See Domingo's opera recording in DVD/VHS format and audio CD for-*

mat.

Domingo has appeared in numerous opera films, among them are Jean-Pierre Ponnelle's *Madama Butterfly*, Gianfranco de Bosio's *Tosca* with Raina Kabaivanska, Giuseppe Patroni Griffi's *Tosca* with Catherine Malfitano (Emmy Award), Franco Zeffirelli's *Cavalleria rusticana & Pagliacci*, all made for television, and, for theatrical release, Francesco Rosi's *Carmen* (Grammy Award for Best Opera Recording), Zeffirelli's *Otello* with Katia Ricciarelli, and Zeffirelli's *La traviata* (with Teresa Stratas, which received a Grammy Award for Best Opera Recording).

His singing voice was heard performing the song "In Pace", during the closing credits of Kenneth Branagh's *Hamlet* (1996).

He has also appeared on television in the 1978 La Scala production of Puccini's *Manon Lescaut* which marked the Scala debut of Hungarian soprano Sylvia Sass, as well in zarzuela evenings, and *Live at the Met* telecasts and broadcasts. In 2007, Domingo had a cameo role in *The Simpsons* episode "Homer of Seville", which revolves around Homer Simpson becoming an opera singer. In his cameo, Domingo sang briefly. Domingo appeared on *The Cosby Show* Season 5 as Alberto Santiago, a colleague of Dr Cliff Huxtable. He also sang as the operatic moon in the 2001 film *Moulin Rouge!*.

In 1989, the international television series, 'Return Journey' featured Domingo returning to his home city of Madrid refecting life there whilst recording an album of Zarzuela arias for EMI. The film was directed by Ken MacGregor.

He is the executive producer of the critically acclaimed 1998 Mexican film, *The Other Conquest*, produced by his son Alvaro and directed by Salvador Carrasco, in which Domingo also performs the original aria "Mater Aeterna", composed by Samuel Zyman with lyrics by Carrasco.

### Christmas in Vienna

In 1990, the idea for a Christmas-themed concert, involving the collaboration of Domingo, fellow operatic tenor and friend José Carreras, and pop music legend Diana Ross was first brought up. Vienna was chosen in 1992 to host the event due to its reputation as a capital of music and the particular charm of Austria during Christmas time. The Wiener Symphoniker under the direction of maestro Vjekoslav Šutej provided the orchestral music, and the Gumpoldskirchen Children's Choir provided choral vocals. On 23 December 1992 the first in what would turn out to be a series of *Christmas in Vienna* concerts was seen worldwide by several hundred million people. Plácido Domingo returned to Vienna for many more *Christmas in Vienna* concerts, performing with stars and friends of both pop and classical music, including Dionne Warwick, Charles Aznavour, Sissel Kyrkjebø, Michael Bolton, Sarah Brightman, Riccardo Cocciante, Patricia Kaas, Luciano Pavarotti, Tony Bennett and others.

### Complete repertoire

Perhaps the most versatile of all living tenors, Domingo has sung 128 opera roles and as many as 131 roles overall in Italian, French, German, English, Spanish and Russian. His main repertoire however is Italian (*Otello*, Cavaradossi in *Tosca*, *Don Carlo*, Des Grieux in *Manon Lescaut*, Dick Johnson in *La fanciulla del West*, Radames in *Aida*), French (*Faust*, *Werther*, Don José in *Carmen*, Samson in *Samson et Dalila*), and German (*Lohengrin*, *Parsifal*, and Siegmund in *Die Walküre*). He continues to add more roles to his repertoire, the latest was the title, baritone role in Verdi's *Simon Boccanegra* on 24 October 2009 at Berlin State Opera. Additionally, Domingo has created several new roles in modern operas, such as the title role in Tan Dun's opera *The First Emperor* at the Metropolitan Opera. In September 2010, he will create the role of the poet Pablo Neruda in the world première of Daniel Catán's opera based on the film *Il Postino* at Los Angeles Opera. During the 2011-2012 Season at the Met he will create the role of Neptune in the original baroque pastiche *The Enchanted Island* conducted by William Christie with a libretto by Jeremy Sams.

### Awards and honors

Plácido Domingo won his first Grammy Award in 1971 and went on to win eight more, as well as three Latin Grammy awards. A Kammersänger of the Vienna State Opera and the recipient of numerous honorary doctorates, his other major awards include an Honorary Knighthood from Queen Elizabeth II of the United Kingdom, Austria's Österreichisches Ehrenzeichen für Wissenschaft und Kunst, France's Ordre national de la Légion d'honneur, Mexico's Orden del Águila Azteca, Spain's Premio Príncipe de Asturias, and the United States Presidential Medal of Freedom.

- A new book by Domingo, *The Joy of Opera*, will be published by W. W. Norton & Company in year 2009

### Humanitarian works and initiatives

- In June 2010 Domingo became President of Europa Nostra, the Voice of Cultural Heritage in Europe
- On 4 March 2006, Domingo sang at the Gala Benefit Concert, "A Night For New Orleans" at the New Orleans Arena to help rebuilding the city after it was hit by Hurricane Katrina. At the gala, he made a statement: "If music be the food of love", then "MUSIC IS THE VOICE OF HOPE!" . On 23 March 2008, the New Orleans City Council named the city theatre's stage in the Mahalia Jackson Theatre in Louis Armstrong Park, the "Plácido Domingo stage" as the honour for his contribution at the Gala Benefits Concert. The Gala collected $700,000 for the city recovery fund.
- In 1986, he performed at benefit concerts to raise funds for the victims of 1985 Mexico City earthquake and released an album of one of the events. On 21 August 2007, as recognition to his support to 1985 Mexico City earthquake victims as well as his artistic works, a statue in his honor, made in Mexico City from

keys donated by the people, was unveiled. The statue is the work of Alejandra Zúñiga, is two meters tall, weighs about 300 kg (660 lbs) and is part of the "Grandes valores" (Great values) program.
- Domingo supports the *Hear the World* initiative as an ambassador to raise awareness for the topic of hearing and hearing loss.
- In 1993 he founded *Operalia, The World Opera Competition*, an international opera competition for talented young singers. The winners get the opportunities of being employed in opera ensembles around the world. Domingo has been instrumental in giving many young artists encouragement, (and special attention) as in 2001, when he invited New York tenor, Daniel Rodriguez to attend the Vilar/Domingo Young Artists program to further develop his operatic skills.
- On 21 December 2003, Domingo made a performance in Cancún to benefit the *Ciudad de la Alegria Foundation*, the foundation that provides assistance and lodging to people in need, including low-income individuals, orphans, expectant mothers, immigrants, rehabilitated legal offenders, and the terminally ill.
- On 27 June 2007, Domingo and Katherine Jenkins performed in a charity concert in Athens to raise funds to aid the conflict in Darfur. The concert was organized by *Medecins Sans Frontieres/Doctors Without Borders*.
- In 2 October 2007, Domingo joins several other preeminent figures in entertainment, government, the environment and more, as the one of receivers of the BMW Hydrogen 7, designed in the mission to build support of hydrogen as a viable substitute to fossil fuels.
- On 17 January 2009 he performed with the New Orleans Opera directed by Robert Lyall in a gala reopening of New Orleans' Mahalia Jackson Theatre for the Performing Arts. The master of ceremonies was New Orleans native Patricia Clarkson.

Source (edited): "http://en.wikipedia.org/wiki/Pl%C3%A1cido_Domingo"

## Ainhoa Arteta

**Ainhoa Arteta Ibarrolaburu**, born 24 September 1964 in Tolosa (Guipúzcoa), Spain, is a Spanish soprano.

**Biography**

After studying in Tolosa and Italy, she later studied under Ruth Falcon.

After winning the Metropolitan Opera National Council Auditions in 1993, her debut at the Metropolitan Opera House in October 1994 was as Mimì in *La Bohème*. She has also performed at the Metropolitan Opera with Plácido Domingo and Mirella Freni and in Poulenc's *Les Mamelles de Tirésias* directed by James Levine.

She was accompanied by Plácido Domingo for her debut at London's Covent Garden.

For her Carnegie Hall debut she was accompanied by Dolora Zajick and Plácido Domingo, with whom she has toured several countries.

She has also performed at Bayerische Staatsoper in Munich, Amsterdam Opera, Bonn Opera, Teatro Bellas Artes in México, Teatro di San Carlo, Washington Opera (La Rondine), San Francisco Opera, Arena di Verona, among others.

She has performed *Faust* at the Bayrische Staatsoper and Münchner Opern-Festspiele with Rolando Villazón, directed by Friedrich Haider.

She has sung with the Orquesta de Cadaqués conducted by Sir Neville Marriner, with Michael Tilson Thomas and the New World Symphony Orchestra.

She has also performed and recorded with her former husband Dwayne Croft.

Among other awards, she has the Concours International de Voix d'Opera Plácido Domingo (Paris).

In December 2008 she gave a series of recitals accompanied by Malcolm Martineau.

**Recordings**

- 1999: *En Concierto* - Ainhoa Arteta and Dwayne Croft with the Orquestra Sinfonica de Castilla y Léon, Bragado Darman, cond. RTVE MUSICA 65126 - recorded live on August 9, 1999 at the Palacio de los Festivales in Cantabria, Spain
- 1999 ' 'La Rondine' ' - Magda - Washington Opera, Decca DVD

Source (edited): "http://en.wikipedia.org/wiki/Ainhoa_Arteta"

## Alexey Kudrya

**Alexey Kudrya** (born 1982) is a rising operatic lyric tenor star from Russia. According to *Neue Stimmen*, Alexey Kudrya grew up in a very musical family: His father, *Vladimir Leonidovich Kudrya*, is professor for music and his mother teaches the flute. Alexey was taught by his father at Moscow's Russian Academy of Music and graduated in 2004 as flautist and conductor.

He began his musical career playing flute. As a flute player he was laureate of several internationals contests. His voice career began with the international competition "Romance 2003" in Moscow where he won the first prize and the special award "Potential of the Nation". He still plays flute on stage, for example, when he performs Prince Tamino in *The Magic Flute* opera by Mozart.

Noting on his tenor style, Benjamin Ivry in The New York Sun commented: "Russia's Alexey Kudrya, who has won medals in several vocal competitions, has a refined lyric voice ideal for recordings and smaller opera houses."

His first engagements in his native Russia took him to the Stanislavsky Theatre in Moscow, also known as Stanislavski and Nemirovich-Danchenko Moscow Academic Music Theatre, as Guest Opera Soloist, where he sang Prince Gvidon in Rimsky-Korsakov's "The Tale of Tsar Saltan", Nemorino in *L'elisir d'amore*, and Ferrando in *Così fan tutte*. At the Stanislavsky Theatre he also studied the parts of Alfredo Germont (*La Traviata*) and Lensky (*Eugene Onegin*). In 2006, he also sang under the baton of Teodor Currentzis in concert performances in Moscow and Novosibirsk to mark the occasion of the 250th anniversary of Mozart's birth.

CommandOpera exclaims that "Alexey Kudrya is the most exciting Russian Tenor on the planet today: his vocal instrument positively 'weeps' in the most Italianate fashion."

## Performances and Competitions

In October 2005 Alexey Kudrya became a laureate of the prestigious international competition "*Neue Stimmen*" (2nd prize). In the Final Concert of "*Neue Stimmen*" competition on 22 October 2005, Alexey Kudrya sang the arias "Kuda, kuda" from *Eugene Onegin* by Peter Tschaikowsky and "*Lunge da lei*" from *La traviata* by Giuseppe Verdi.

In 2005-2006 he continued to improve his vocal skills in Galina Vishnevskaya's Opera Centre.

In 2006, he debuted in Europe singing Lensky's aria from *Eugene Onegin* at I International Opera Singers Competition of Galina Vishnevskaya (2nd prize). Further, he was described as the audience favorite, whose tenor is in the lyrical mold of past Russians as Ivan Kozlovsky and Sergei Lemeshev, fluent and expressive, but with a welcome element of *vitality*. Aside from singing, he also performed the unusual feat of accompanying his stylish vocal account of "*Wie stark ist nicht dein Zauberton*", from *Die Zauberflöte*, on the flute.

In 2007, he won the "*Iris Adami Corradetti International Competition*" of Opera Singing.

In 2009, he won 1st prize in Placido Domingo's world famous "*Operalia*" Competition held in Hungary, and as well as the Special Prize offered by the Hungarian State Opera. In the same competition, the 1st prize award forsoprano was *Julia Novikova (soprano)*, also from Russia.

Same year March-April 2009, he performed *Ferrando* in *Così fan tutte*, at *Vlaamse Opera House* in Netherlands; a *Dramma Giocoso* in two acts by Wolfgang Amadeus Mozart (1756–1791) based on a libretto by Lorenzo Da Ponte.

2010/11 marks his debut at the Vienna State opera, where he will sing Almaviva in "*Il barbiere di Siviglia*" in December/January. This role will also mark his debut at the MET in September/October 2011.

Other commitments this 2010/11 season include
- Productions of "Zauberflöte" with the St. Margarethen Festival, Austria
- "Il barbiere di Siviglia" in Palermo
- "L'elisir d'amore" and "Barbiere" in Budapest
- "I puritani" in Geneva
- "Linda di Chamounix" in Toulon
- "Don Giovanni" in Marseille
- "Don Pasquale" in Washington

Source (edited): "http://en.wikipedia.org/wiki/Alexey_Kudrya"

# Ana María Martínez

**Ana María Martínez** is a Grammy award winning operatic soprano from Puerto Rico. "The most beautiful voice of Latin America", (BZ Berlin) [Martínez] "requires ranking among the top lyric sopranos of the day...[with] immaculate musicality underpinning every utterance." (Opera Magazine)

## Early life

Ana María Martínez was born in San Juan, Puerto Rico, the daughter of Puerto Rican opera singer Evangelína Colón and Dr. Ángel Martínez, a Cuban psychoanalyst. Martínez can trace her grandparents back to Spain and France before coming to the Caribbean Islands. Martínez grew up with discipline and experienced a strict Catholic upbringing.

## Career

Highlights of Ms. Martinez's illustrious career include her debut with the Metropolitan Opera as Micaëla in *Carmen* for which Marion Lignana Rosenberg of Newsday said: "A lovely singer, Martínez is something more rare and wonderful besides: a beautiful musician. She shades her smoky, soft-grained voice with finesse, phrasing with unfussy grace and serving up some of the most ravishing soft singing heard at the Met in years. " For her debut in the title role of *Rusalka* at the Glyndebourne Festival she was praised for her "brave back-flips before singing a radiant 'Song to the Moon'. Her dusky lyric soprano rides the great closing scene to heartbreaking effect." (Sunday Telegraph) Ms. Martinez's debut performance with the Opera de Bastille was as Amelia in a new production of *Simon Boccanegra*, and she returned there to sing the title role in a new production of Verdi's *Luisa Miller*. Performances at the Royal Opera House Convent Garden include Donna Elvira in *Don Giovanni* and at the Bayerische Staatsoper in Munich the title role of *Luisa Miller* and the Countess in *Le Nozze di Figaro*.

An alumna of the Houston Grand Opera Studio, Ms. Martiez has appeared in numerous productions with the Opera house, including her performance as Lucero in the World Premier of Daniel Catán's *Salsipuedes*, Mimi in *La Boheme*, Donna Elvira in *Don Giovanni*, La Contessa in *Le Nozze di Figaro*, and Liù in *Turandot*. At the San Francisco Opera she has performed as Amelia in *Simon Boccanegra*, Micaëla in *Carmen*, and Pamina in the *Die Zauberflöte*. In addition, she has had leading roles with the Netherlands Opera, Los Angeles Opera, Santa Fe Opera, Dresden Semper Opera, Vienna Staatsoper, Seattle Opera, Staatsoper Stuttgart, Oper der Stadt Bonn, Deutsche Oper Berlin, Hamburg Opera, New York City Opera, Washington National Opera, and the Seattle Opera.

Ms. Martinez continually inspires audiences from the concert stage, with notable appearances including world tours with Andrea Bocelli and Placido Domingo, as well as performances with the SWR Sinfonieorchester Baden-Baden und Freiburg, Orchestre de Paris, Berlin Philharmonic Orchestra, the Boston Symphony at Carnegie Hall, and the Puerto Rico Symphony at the Kennedy Center. Festival appearances include performances at the Ravinia Festival, Tuscan Sun Festival in Cortona, Italy, Salzburg Festival, Florence Maggio Musicale Festival, and the Casals Festival in Puerto Rico. She has worked with such distinguished conductors as Placido Domingo, Sylvan Cambreling, Gustavo Dudamel, Bernard Haitink, and Giuseppe Sinopoli, among others.

Her solo recording, simply titled *Ana María Martínez – Soprano Songs and Arias*, recorded with the Prague Philharmonia conducted by Steven Mercurio on Naxos, was released to critical acclaim and selected by Gramophone Magazine as an "Editor's Choice." She stars on the Decca DVD *Cosi Fan Tutte* filmed at the Salzburg Festival and performs the role of Nedda opposite Andrea Bocelli in the Universal CD recording of *I Pagliacci* which debuted at #1. She can also be seen on the EuroArts DVD *Spanish Night* recorded with the Berlin Philharmonic conducted by Placido Domingo.

Her discography also includes a performance on Steven Mercurio's Sony Classical CD, *Many Voices*, and the Latin Grammy award-winning recording of Albeniz's *Merlin* with Plácido Domingo (Decca), which coincided with the Grammy nominated recording of Bacalov's *Misa Tango* with Plácido Domingo (Deutsche Grammophon).

Additional recordings include Glass' *La Belle et la Bête* and *Symphony No. 5* (Nonesuch), Albeniz's *Henry Clifford* (Decca), Joaquin Rodrigo's *Obra Vocal I, II, IV & V* (EMI), and Daniel Catán's *Florencia en el Amazonas* (Albany). Recorded on Naxos for the Milken Archives and with the Academy of St. Martin-in-the-Fields, she can be heard on Castelnuovo Tedesco's *Naomi & Ruth Opus 27* (Naxos) as well as Yizkor's *Requiem* (Naxos) and with the Barcelona Symphony, Marvin Levy's *Canto de los Marranos* (Naxos), Julius Chajes' *Old Jerusalem* (Naxos) and Hugo Weisgall's *Psalm of the Distant Dove* (Naxos). Her rendition of "Ave Maria" is heard in the Denzel Washington film "John Q" and she has been featured on the Emmy nominated PBS TV special and DVD "American Dream: Andrea Bocelli's Statue of Liberty Concert" with the New Jersey Symphony and she joins Placido Domingo for a DVD of Zarzuelas entitled *Amor, Vida de Mi Vida*, which was recorded live with the Mozarteum Orchestra Salzburg.

A graduate of the Juilliard School with Bachelor and Master of Music degrees and alumna of the Houston Grand Opera Studio, Martinez won the Pepita Embil Award at the 1995 Operalia II, first prize in the 1994 Eleanor McCollum Auditions and Awards from Houston Grand Opera, and in the 1993 Metropolitan Opera National Council Auditions she was a first place district and first place regional winner and national finalist.

## Personal life

Martínez met her husband, tenor Chad Shelton, while working at Houston Grand Opera and the two have often sung together on the HGO stage. They have one son together, born in 2007.

## Awards

Martínez has won prizes including the Pepita Embil Award, the Plácido Domingo International Voice Competition, and first prize at the Eleanor McCollum Awards.

Martínez won a Latin Grammy in 2001 for Classical Album for Isaac Albéniz's *Merlin* with Carlos Álvarez, Plácido Domingo, Jane Henschel and conductor José De Eusebio with the Orquesta Sinfónica de Madrid.

## Discography

- *Soprano Songs and Arias: Ana María Martínez*, Naxos, 2005
- *Dvorak: Rusalka*, Glyndebourne, 2010
- *Amor, Vida de mi Vida*, (DVD) Euroarts, 2009
- *American Classics – Beveridge/ Marriner for the Milken Archive of American Jewish Music*, Naxos, 2005
- *Weisgall: T'Kiatot Rituals for Rosh Hashana*, Naxos, 2004
- *Levy: Masada (Canto de Los Marranos) for the Milken Archive of American Jewish Music*, Naxos, 2004
- *Introducing the World of American Jewish Music for the Milken Archive of American Jewish Music*, Naxos, 2003
- *Castelnuovo – Tedesco: Naomi & Ruth*, Naxos, 2003
- *Spanish Night from the Berlin Waldbühne*, (DVD) Naxos, 2003
- *Rodrigo: 100 Años – La Obra Vocal, I y II*, EMI, 2002
- *Rodrigo: 100 Años – La Obra Vocal, IV y V*, EMI, 2002
- *Albéniz: Henry Clifford*, Decca, 2003
- *Albéniz: Merlin*, Decca, 2000
- *Catan: Florencia en el Amazonas*, Albany, 2003
- *Glass: Philip on Film*, (Box Set) Nonesuch, 2001
- *Glass: Symphony No. 5*, Nonesuch, 2000
- *Glass: La Belle et la Bête*, Nonesuch, 1995
- *Bacalov: Misa Tango*, Deutsche Grammophon, 2000
- *Sheng: The Song of Majnun – A Persian Romeo and Juliet*, Delos, 1997
- *American Dream: Andrea Bocelli's Statue of Liberty Concert*, (TV/DVD) WNET/THIRTEEN, 2000
- *Mozart: Così fan tutte*, (DVD) Decca, 2007
- *Leoncavallo: Pagliacci*, Decca, 2007
- *Mercurio: Many Voices*, Sony, 2006

Source (edited): "http://en.wikipedia. org/wiki/Ana_Mar%C3%ADa_Mart% C3%ADnez"

# Andión Fernández

**Andión Fernández** is a Spanish-Philippine operatic soprano, born in Manila.

A soloist of the Deutsche Oper Berlin since 2001, she graduated with honors from the Hochschule der Künste, Berlin, and has studied voice with Karan Armstrong and Ira Hartmann, and contemporary music with Aribert Reimann. She is a prizewinner of Operalia International Opera Competition (Placido Domingo World Opera Contest, Hamburg) and the Cardiff Singer of the World competition. The major international opera houses she has sung in include the Deutsche Oper Berlin, the Deutsche Oper am Rhein, the Deutsche Staatsoper Berlin, the Nuremberg Opera, the Gulbenkian Auditorium in Lisbon, the Festwochen Herrenhausen in Hannover, the Schloß Sanssouci in Potsdam, the Kallang Theatre and Victoria Theatre in Singapore, the Festspielhaus in Baden Baden, and the Gran Teatre del Liceu in Barcelona. Among her major roles are Susanna (*Le nozze di Figaro*), Niklausse (*Les contes d'Hoffmann*), Hänsel (*Hänsel und Gretel*), Micaela (*Carmen*), Fox (*The Cunning Little Vixen*), and Pamina (*Die Zauberflöte*). She has worked with many distinguished conductors, including Alberto Zedda, Christian Thielemann, Marcello Viotti, Kent Nagano, Christopher Hogwood, Leopold Hager, and Mikhail Jurowski. As Agnes in Mikhail Jurowski's world premiere recording of Emil von Reznicek's *Ritter Blaubart* she received rave reviews. She is married to the composer Jeffrey Ching, and sang the solo part in his *Symphony No. 5, "Kunstkammer"* at its world premiere under Mikhail Jurowski in March 2006. She will sing the title role in Ching's new opera *The Orphan*, commissioned by Theater Erfurt, Germany, for its 2009-2010 season.

Source (edited): "http://en.wikipedia. org/wiki/Andi%C3%B3n_Fern%C3% A1ndez"

# Angel Blue

**Angel Joy Blue** (born May 3, 1983 in California) is an American operatic soprano. Blue's voice has been recognized for its shining and agile upper register, "smoky" middle register, and beautiful timbre. She has performed internationally and won numerous awards such as Operalia and Miss Hollywood. Placido Domingo has described Angel as "the next Leontyne Price".

## Career

Angel Blue has performed lead roles and as a featured soloist at Los Angeles Opera, San Francisco Opera, Walt Disney Concert Hall, the Colburn School, Royce Hall, the Staples Center, Auditorio Nacional de Música, Seoul Arts Center.

Her operatic repertoire includes such roles as Violetta (La Traviata), Musetta (La Boheme), Micaela (Carmen), Lucia (Lucia di Lammermoor), Helena (A Midsummer Night's Dream), Liu (Turandot), Manon (Manon), Contessa Almaviva (Le Nozze di Figaro), Olympia and Antonia (Tales of Hoffmann), Dido (Dido and Aeneas), and Donna Anna (Don Giovanni).

Blue has sung the National Anthem for the Border Governors Conference, hosted by California Governor Arnold Schwarzenegger, and for the California Women's Conference, hosted by California First Lady Maria Shriver.

## Awards

In 2009, Ms. Blue was a finalist in Operalia, receiving 1st place in the Zarzuela competition, and 2nd place in the Opera competition. She has also received awards from the Metropolitan Opera National Council Auditions, the Dorothy Chandler Pavilion's Emerging Young Entertainers Award, and the Redlands Bowl Competition.

## Education

Blue received a Masters of Music degree in Opera Performance from UCLA in 2007 and a Bachelor's of Music from the University of Redlands in 2005. She is an alumnus of the Los Angeles County High School for the Arts where she studied voice and classical piano. She was a member of the Domingo-Thornton Young Artist Program at Los Angeles Opera from 2007/2009. Angel is a current member of the Artistas de la Academia "Placido Domingo" del Palau de les Arts from 2009–2010, under Maestros Alberto Zedda, Lorin Maazel, and Zubin Mehta.

## Causes

Angel Blue has been a featured soloist on the Madrilenos por Haiti concert with La Orquesta Clasica de Espana in Madrid, Spain. The concert was dedicated to raising funds for housing projects for Haitians who have relocated to the Dominican Republic.

## Pageants

In addition to singing, the 5'11" soprano is a former model and beauty queen. Blue was the first and only African-American to have held the title of Miss Apple Valley California. She competed in the Miss Empire America pageant and received 1st runner in 2003. She has held such titles as Miss Hollywood 2005, Miss Southern California 2006, and 1st runner up to both Miss California 2006 and Miss Nevada 2007 and finished 1st runner up at Miss California 2005. In 2005 Angel represented the state of California as Miss California Sweetheart at the National Sweetheart Pageant, where she won the overall tal-

## Arturo Chacón Cruz

Arturo Chacón-Cruz

**Arturo Chacón-Cruz** (August 20, 1977) is a Mexican operatic tenor. A winner of the Operalia competition in 2005, he went on to sing leading roles at many North American opera houses, including Los Angeles Opera, Washington National Opera, and Houston Grand Opera. He has also appeared in many European opera houses, including the Teatro Real in Madrid, La Fenice in Venice, and the Berlin State Opera.
Chacón-Cruz was born in Cd. Obregon, Sonora, raised in Navojoa, Sonora.

He has been acclaimed for his portrayal of Rodolfo in *La Bohème*, due to the youthfulness, beauty and power of his voice, as well as his sincere interpretation of the role. A graduate of the prestigious Houston Grand Opera Studio, he also graduated form numerous institutions, including SIVAM workshops, the Boston University's Opera Institute and San Francisco Opera's Merola Opera Program.

He did his Palacio de Bellas Artes debut (Mexico City) in 1999, in the "III Gala Latina" and he has returned several times to that stage for many concerts and Opera.

He made his Carnegie Hall debut in March 2002 singing in Mozart's Coronation Mass, he later returned to Carnegie Hall in June 2003 to sing Beethoven's *Mass in C* and Charpentier's *Te Deum* with the New England Symphonic Ensemble, as well a concert with the New York Pops in 2006.

He made his debut with the San Francisco Symphony Orchestra as part of the "Summer in the City" concert series in July 2004. In September 2005 he sang a concert of Mexican songs and Spanish music with the Houston Symphony Orchestra. As well he debuts with the Montreal Symphony Orchestra in 2008, under the baton of Maestro Kent Nagano performing the Tenor solo in the Verdi Requiem during the Lanaudière Festival in Joliette. In 2010, he made his Chinese debut in Beijing, under the baton of Maestro Lorin Maazel, singing Alfredo in La traviata.

Chacón-Cruz has received many awards, including the Antonio Davalos Award in Mexico's Carlo Morelli's competition, First Place and Audience Choice Award at the 2003 Eleanor McCollum Competition in Houston Grand Opera, winner of Metropolitan Opera National Council Auditions in the New England Region, Plácido Domingo's Operalia 2005. He was also the recipient of the Ramón Vargas Opera Grant given by Mr. Vargas and Pro Ópera in Mexico. He was named as well 2006 Artist of the year by El Imparcial Cultural Organization in his hometown of Hermosillo, Mexico.

### Repertoire

Some of his tenor roles include:
- Arcadio in Daniel Catán's *Florencia en el Amazonas*,
- Rodolfo in *La bohème*,
- Pinkerton in *Madama Butterfly*,
- Rinuccio in *Gianni Schicchi*,
- Ruggero in *La Rondine*,
- Lensky in Tchaikovsky's *Eugene Onegin*,
- Alfredo in *La traviata*,
- Il Duca di Mantova in *Verdi's Rigoletto*,
- The Tenor solo in the *Verdi Requiem*,
- Romeo and Faust in Gounod's *Roméo et Juliette* and *Faust*,
- Christian in Alfano's *Cyrano de Bergerac*,
- The title role in Mozart's *Idomeneo*,
- Tamino in *The Magic Flute*,
- Marcello di Bruges in Donizetti's *Il duca d'Alba*,
- Nemorino in Gaetano Donizetti's *l'Elisir d'Amore*,
- Des Grieux in Massenet's *Manon*,
- the title role in *Werther*,
- the title role in *Les Contes d'Hoffmann*,
- Uriel in Haydn's *The Creation*.

### Venues

- Washington National Opera,
- Houston Grand Opera,
- National Centre for the Performing Arts, Beijing, China,
- Opera Pacific,
- Berlin Staatsoper Unter den Linden,
- Detroit Opera,
- The Keller Auditorium with The Portland Opera,
- Los Angeles Opera,
- Grazer Oper, Austria,
- Oper Köln, Germany,
- Hamburgische Staatsoper, Hamburg, Germany,
- Teatro Comunale di Bologna,
- Teatro di San Carlo,
- Connecticut Opera,
- Cincinnati Opera,
- Palau de les Arts Reina Sofía, Spain,
- Palacio de Bellas Artes, in Mexico,
- Teatro de la Ciudad, in Mexico City,
- Sala Nezahualcoyotl, in Mexico City,
- Teatro Real in Madrid,
- Teatro La Fenice in Venice,
- Teatro Regio di Torino, in Turin,
- Vatroslav Lisinski Concert Hall, Zagreb, Croatia,
- Opéra National de Montpellier and Festival de Radio France,
- the National Theatre of Miskolc in Hungary,
- Carnegie Hall, New York City,

- the Mormon Tabernacle Choir in Salt Lake City,
- Le Corum: Montpellier France,
- Opera de Lyon, Lyon, France,
- Opera Royal de Wallonie, Liege, Belgium,
- National Centre for the Performing Arts (China),
- Aichi Triennale Festival, Nagoya, Japan

**Recordings**
- Marcello di Bruges, "Il duca d'Alba"
- Christian, Cyrano de Bergerac, DVD Release by Naxos Records
- Featured in Renée Fleming's Verismo CD

Source (edited): "http://en.wikipedia.org/wiki/Arturo_Chac%C3%B3n_Cruz"

# Brian Asawa

**Brian Asawa** (born 1966, Los Angeles) is a Japanese-American countertenor.

He began his studies as a piano major at the University of California, Santa Cruz, ultimately switching his studies to singing under tenor Harlan Hokin. After two semesters there he transferred to UCLA where he studied under Virginia Fox and Kari Windingstad. In 1989 he began a masters degree in early-music interpretation at the University of Southern California in Los Angeles where he was a pupil of the British lutanist James Tyler. However, Asawa never finished this program as his performance career began to take off.

The singer's career was launched in 1991 when he became the first countertenor to win both the Metropolitan Opera National Council Auditions and an Adler Fellowship to the San Francisco Opera's Merola Opera Program. He made his professional opera debut at the San Francisco Opera in 1991 in Hans Werner Henze's *Das verratene Meer* where he also sang the Shepherd in *Tosca* and Oberon in Benjamin Britten's *A Midsummer Night's Dream* in 1992. While at the SFO he continued further voice studies with Jane Randolph. He also made his first opera appearance in New York City in 1992 at the Mozart Bicentennial celebration at Lincoln Center, singing the title role in Mozart's *Ascanio in Alba* with the Mostly Mozart Festival Chorus and the New York Chamber Symphony under conductor Ádám Fischer.

In 1993 Asawa was awarded a career grant from the Richard Tucker Music Foundation and that same year made his debut at the Santa Fe Opera as Arsamene in George Frideric Handel's *Xerxes*. In 1994 he became the first countertenor to win the Plácido Domingo Operalia International Opera Competition, and made debuts at the Metropolitan Opera as the Voice of Apollo in Benjamin Britten's *Death in Venice* and Glimmerglass Opera as Ottone in Claudio Monteverdi's *L'incoronazione di Poppea*. He was chosen Seattle Opera's Artist of the Year for the 1996–97 season.

Asawa's other career highlights include Orlofsky in *Die Fledermaus* at San Francisco Opera and San Diego Opera; Tolomeo in *Giulio Cesare* at Metropolitan Opera, Bordeaux, Opera Australia, Royal Opera House, Covent Garden, Paris Opera, Gran Teatre del Liceu in Barcelona, and Hamburg State Opera; Arsamene in *Serse* at Los Angeles, Cologne, Seattle, and Geneva; Admeto in *Admeto* at Sydney, Montpellier and Halle; Baba The Turk in *The Rake's Progress* at San Francisco and for Swedish television; Fyodor in *Boris Godunov* at the Gran Teatre del Liceu, Endimione in La Calisto in Brussels, Oberon in *A Midsummer Night's Dream* at San Francisco, Houston, London Symphony Orchestra and Lyon; Ascanio in *Ascanio in Alba* at the Lincoln Center; Farnace in *Mitridate, re di Ponto* at Opera National de Lyon and Paris Opera; Nero in *L'incoronazione di Poppea* in Sydney; Orfeo in *Orfeo ed Euridice*, La Speranza in *L'Orfeo* and L'Umana Fragilita/Anfinomo in *Il ritorno d'Ulisse in Patria* at Netherlands Opera; David in *Saul* and Belize in *Angels* at the Bavarian State Opera, and Sesto in *Giulio Cesare* at COC in Toronto.

Brian Asawa's discography includes four solo recital discs ranging from Dowland and Edmund Campion to Rachmaninoff and Ned Rorem. Opera recordings include Farnace in *Mitridate* for Decca, Arsamene in *Serse* for Conifer and Oberon in *A Midsummer Night's Dream* for Philips with the London Symphony Orchestra under Sir Colin Davis.

Asawa is the nephew of sculptor Ruth Asawa.

Source (edited): "http://en.wikipedia.org/wiki/Brian_Asawa"

# Carlos Cosías

**Carlos Cosías** is a Spanish operatic tenor born in Barcelona, Spain.

Cosías studied music and piano in the Conservatori Superior de Música del Liceu in Barcelona. He specialised in singing, studying with Jaume Francisco Puig and Eduard Giménez, and working with his regular accompanist, Marco Evangelisti.

His repertoire includes works such as Verdi's Requiem and *La bohème*, and leading roles in bel canto operas such as *Il giovedi grasso*, *Don Pasquale*, *L'elisir d'amore*, *Anna Bolena* and *Lucia di Lammermoor*, which he sang at the Gran Teatre del Liceu in Barcelona and in Cagliari (Italy). He has also performed in *La vida breve*, *Macbeth*, *Canço d'amor i de guerra*, *Il matrimo-*

*nio segreto*, *Gianni Schicchi* (Teatro Arriaga, Bilbao), *Juana de Arco en la hoguera* (Granada Festival), *La bohème* (Nice and Teatro Campoamor, Oviedo), *La traviata* (Teatro Gayarre, Pamplona and Gran Teatre del Liceu) and *Rigoletto* (in Korea). In the sacred music repertoire he has performed as a soloist in Rossini's *Petite Messe Solennelle* and Mozart's *Coronation Mass*.

Amongst his performances in the 2008/2009 season were role debuts as the Duke of Mantua in *Rigoletto* at the Croatian National Theater, and as Don Ottavio in *Don Giovanni* at the Teatre de La Farándula in Sabadell.

### Awards
- Manuel Ausensi Singing Competition in Barcelona (1998)
- Plácido Domingo-Pepita Embil Prize for the Best Zarzuela Singer at Operalia, The World Opera Competition (1998)
- Second place at the International Competition Francesc Viñas
- The Best Singer of Donizetti and Best Spanish Singer at the International Competition Francesc Viñas

Source (edited): "http://en.wikipedia.org/wiki/Carlos_Cos%C3%ADas"

# David Bižić

David Bizic.

**David Bižić** (Serbian Cyrillic: Давид Бижић ) (born 25 November 1975) is an operatic baritone. He was born in Belgrade, Serbia.

## Career

He studied singing with Bibiana Goldenthal at the Jerusalem Academy of Music and Dance and received scholarships from the International Vocal Arts Institute (IVAI) and the America Israel Cultural Foundation (AICF). He has participated in numerous master classes and concerts in France, Israel, New York and Japan working with José van Dam, Teresa Berganza and Gabriel Bacquier among others.

In The Israeli Opera he sang the role of Jake Wallace (*La fanciulla del West* / Puccini), the King (*Aida* / Verdi) and the High Priest (*Nabucco* / Verdi). With IVAI he sang The Father (*Hänsel und Gretel* / Humperdinck), Masetto (*Don Giovanni* / Mozart), Sancho (*Don Quichotte* / Massenet), Hali (*L'italiana in Algeri* / Rossini) and Belcore (*L'elisir d'amore* / Donizetti).

In 2003, David Bizic became a member of the Opera Studio of Paris National Opera and took part in many productions of the Opéra Bastille and the Opera Garnier: Anführer der Prevote (*Cardillac* / Hindemith), Steuermann (*Tristan und Isolde* / Wagner), Metivier (*War and Peace* / Prokofiev), Berger (*Pelléas et Mélisande* / Debussy), Vecchio Zingaro (*Il trovatore* / Verdi), Frere Ruffin (*St. François d'Assise* / Messiaen), Chekunov (*From the House of the Dead* / Janáček), which he repeated in Teatro Real in Madrid.

In 2006, Masetto (*Don Giovanni* / Mozart) in Opera Garnier. Belcore (*L'elisir d'amore* / Donizetti) in Belgrade National Opera, Figaro (*Le nozze di Figaro* / Mozart ) in Opera Angers and Nantes], Manuel (*La vida breve* / De Falla) with Orchestre de Paris in Theatre Mogador in Paris, Creon (*Oedipus rex* / Stravinsky) and Chamberlain (*Le Rossignol* / Stravinsky) in Strasbourg Opéra national du Rhin.

In 2007 he made debut in Toulouse at the Théâtre du Capitole with Leporello (*Don Giovanni* / Mozart) and won the 2nd prize in prestigious Plácido Domingo Operalia Competition.

In 2008, High Priest of Dagon (*Samson et Dalila* / Saint-Saëns) in Royal Swedish Opera and Figaro (*Le nozze di Figaro* / Mozart) in Strasbourg Opéra national du Rhin

In 2009, Leporello (*Don Giovanni* / Mozart) in Opera Rennes, Publio (*La clemenza di Tito* / Mozart) in Avignon, and Schaunard (*La bohème*) and Mathieu (*Andrea Chénier*) in Opéra Bastille

In 2010, Figaro in Opéra de Monte-Carlo, Masetto (*Don Giovanni* / Mozart) in Festival d'Aix-en-Provence, Leporello (*Don Giovanni* / Mozart) in Bolshoi Theatre in Moscow, Escamillo (*Carmen* / Bizet) in National Theatre in Belgrade

His future engagements include Leporello in Deutsche Oper Berlin, Schaunard (La bohème) in Covent Garden, Royal Opera House, Aeneas (Dido and Aeneas) in Toulon Opera, Leporello in Opéra Bastille, Figaro in Grand Théâtre de Bordeaux and Escamillo (Carmen / Bizet) in Royal Swedish Opera

Source (edited): "http://en.wikipedia.org/wiki/David_Bi%C5%BEi%C4%87"

# Elizabeth Futral

Elizabeth Futral

**Elizabeth Futral** (b. 1963, North Carolina) is an American coloratura soprano who has won acclaim throughout the United States as well as in Europe, South America, and Japan.

Raised in Covington, Louisiana, Futral earned a bachelor's degree in music performance from Samford University. After studying with Virginia Zeani at Indiana University, she spent two years as an apprentice with the Lyric Opera of Chicago. She first garnered acclaim in the title role of the 1994 New York City Opera production of Delibes' *Lakmé*. Edward Rothstein wrote in *The New York Times*: "Ms Futral's performance was crucial to the success of the evening.... Ms Futral was refined and accurate, hitting her high notes without strain or artifice, giving her vocal acrobatics warmth without ever succumbing to egoism. She was not out to prove anything; the song ['The Bell Song'] was not laden with excessive emotion or elaborate musical gestures: it had the virtues of her performance throughout the evening, offering simplicity, grace and directness." In 1995 Futral won 2nd Prize in Plácido Domingo's Operalia International Opera Competition. In 1996 she was invited to the Rossini Opera Festival to sing the title role in the first production of Rossini's *Matilde di Shabran* since 1821. Later that year, she sang the role of Catherine in Meyerbeer's *L'étoile du nord* at the Wexford Festival.

In September 1998, she created the role of Stella in the world premiere of André Previn's *A Streetcar Named Desire* for the San Francisco Opera. In February 2001, she debuted with the Los Angeles Opera as Cleopatra in Handel's *Giulio Cesare*. Other roles she has sung for the Los Angeles Opera include Sophie in Strauss's *Der Rosenkavalier* and Violetta in Verdi's *La traviata*.

On January 8, 1999, Futral made her debut with the Metropolitan Opera in the title role of Donizetti's *Lucia di Lammermoor*. In 2003, she sang the role of Princess Eudoxie in the Met's first performances of Halévy's *La Juive* since 1936. She returned to the Met in December 2006 to star opposite Plácido Domingo and Paul Groves in the world premiere of Tan Dun's *The First Emperor*, later appearing in *I puritani*. In 2009 she portrayed Laura Jesson in the world premiere of Houston Grand Opera's production of André Previn's *Brief Encounter* with Nathan Gunn as Alec Harvey.

The soprano's recordings include *Six Characters in Search of an Author*, *L'étoile du nord*, *A Streetcar Named Desire*, *Otello* (of Rossini), *Lucia di Lammermoor* (in English translation), *Of Mice and Men* (of Floyd), *Zelmira*, *Orpheus & Euridice* (of Gordon), as well as "Sweethearts" (on Newport Classic).

Futral and her husband, noted conductor and artistic director of Opera Roanoke Steven White, live in Franklin County, Virginia, near Roanoke.

Source (edited): "http://en.wikipedia.org/wiki/Elizabeth_Futral"

# Eric Owens (bass-baritone)

Julie Taymor, Eric Owens as Grendel, Elliot Goldenthal, and Salma Hayek - credit Robert Millard

**Eric Owens** is an American operatic bass-baritone born July 11, 1970 in Philadelphia. He attended Central High School (Philadelphia, Pennsylvania) "247", Temple University's Boyer College of Music, and the Curtis Institute in Philadelphia. Owens has performed both in new works and reinterpreted classic repertoire.

## Awards

- 2003 Marian Anderson Award,
- First prize in the Plácido Domingo Operalia Competition

## Career

- San Francisco Opera debut as Lodovico in *Otello*
- Royal Opera, Covent Garden debut as Oroveso in *Norma*
- Los Angeles Opera debut as Ferrando in *Il Trovatore*
- Houston Grand Opera as Ramfis in *Aida*
- Metropolitan Opera as General Leslie Groves in Doctor Atomic

He created the title roles of General Leslie Groves in the world premiere of John Adams' *Doctor Atomic* at the San Francisco Opera in 2005; Grendel in Elliot Goldenthal's opera of the same name in the world premiere at the Los Angeles Opera in 2006; and later the same year as the Storyteller in the world premiere of Adams' *A Flowering Tree* at Peter Sellars' New Crowned Hope Festival in Vienna. *A Flowering Tree* recorded with the London Symphony Orchestra on the Nonesuch label is available on CD.

Eric Owens will play Alberich in the Metropolitan Opera's new production of Wagner's Ring Cycle in September

2010. He will be featured in the upcoming CD, "Great Strauss Scenes" on July 27, 2010.

Source (edited): "http://en.wikipedia.org/wiki/Eric_Owens_(bass-baritone)"

# Erwin Schrott

**Erwin Schrott** (born 21 December 1972 in Montevideo, Uruguay) is an operatic bass-baritone, particularly known for his interpretation of the title role in Mozart's *Don Giovanni*.

## Career

Schrott studied singing with Franca Mattiucci. He made his professional debut in Montevideo at the age of 22, singing Roucher in *Andrea Chénier*. Following a stint at the Teatro Municipal in Santiago, Chile, where he sang Timur in *Turandot*, Colline in *La bohème*, Sparafucile in *Rigoletto* and Ramfis in *Aida*, he won a scholarship to study in Italy.

After winning First Prize (Male Singer) and the Audience Prize in the 1998 Operalia competition founded by Plácido Domingo, he went on to leading roles in major opera houses in both Europe and the United States. He made his debut at the Vienna State Opera as Banquo in Verdi's *Macbeth* on 28 March 1999 and returned there to sing Leporello in *Don Giovanni* and Figaro in *Le nozze di Figaro*. At La Scala he has sung the title role in *Don Giovanni* and Pharaon in *Moïse et Pharaon*. His debut at the New York Metropolitan Opera came on 30 November 2000 when he sang Colline in *La bohème*. He returned to the company in 2005 as Escamillo in *Carmen*, in 2006 in the title role in *Don Giovanni* for the Met's Japan Tour, in 2007 as Figaro in *Le nozze di Figaro* and in 2008 in the title role in *Don Giovanni*. Since his debut at the Royal Opera House in September 2003 as Leporello in *Don Giovanni*, Schrott has sung Figaro in *Le nozze di Figaro*, and the title role in *Don Giovanni* with the company.

Erwin Schrott's performances on the concert stage include a joint concert with Anna Netrebko conducted by Plácido Domingo in the Centro de Bellas Artes, San Juan, Puerto Rico (9 October 2007), a gala concert for the 5th Abu Dhabi Music and Arts Festival, with Anna Netrebko and Elīna Garanča (29 March 2008), and a solo concert in the Münchner Residenz (9 November 2008).

## Personal life

Erwin Schrott is married to the Russian soprano Anna Netrebko. Their son, Tiago Aruã, was born on 5 September 2008 in Vienna. In addition to their joint concerts in Puerto Rico, Abu Dhabi and Riga, Netrebko and Schrott have appeared together in *Don Giovanni* with the New York Metropolitan Opera's Japan Tour in June 2006 and at the Royal Opera House in June 2007.

In April 2008, concert promoter Ian Rosenblatt said that he was planning to sue Schrott for breach of contract when he cancelled his appearance in the Rosenblatt Recital Series for 11 June 2008 at Cadogan Hall. The dispute was settled out of court in August 2008 when Schrott agreed to make a donation to charity.

## Recordings

- *Le nozze di Figaro* (Mozart) Royal Opera House, 2008, Antonio Pappano conducting. Opus Arte, DVD & Blu-ray
- *L'elisir d'amore* (Dulcamara), Macerata Opera Festival, 2002, Niels Muus conducting. Rai Trade DVD and CD
- *Moïse et Pharaon* (Pharaon), Teatro alla Scala, 2003, Riccardo Muti conducting. TDK DVD
- *Arias by Mozart, Verdi, Berlioz, Gounod & Meyerbeer*, 2008, Orquestra de la Comunitat Valenciana, Riccardo Frizza conducting. Decca CD

Source (edited): "http://en.wikipedia.org/wiki/Erwin_Schrott"

# Giuseppe Filianoti

Giuseppe Filianoti

**Giuseppe Filianoti** (born 11 January 1974) is an Italian lyric tenor from Reggio Calabria.

### Early years
Born in 1974, the Italian tenor obtained his degree in Literature from the Università Degli Studi di Messina, in the Sicilian town of Messina. In 1997, he graduated from the 'Francesco Cilea' Conservatory in his hometown, studying under Anna Vandi. Filianoti then won a prestigious two-year scholarship to the Accademia del Teatro alla Scala in Milan. It was during this time that he met Alfredo Kraus, who became his mentor and his decisive influence in artistic approach, nuance, technique, and style.

### Career
Filianoti made his professional début in 1998 at Bergamo in the title role of *Dom Sébastien*, by Gaetano Donizetti. In 1999, after singing Argirio in *Tancredi* at the Rossini Opera Festival in Pesaro, he was engaged by Riccardo Muti to sing in Paisello's *Nina, o sia La pazza per amore* with La Scala. In 2003, again under Muti, he opened the season of La Scala with Rossini's *Moïse et Pharaon*, and with La Scala and Daniel Barenboim he has performed the Verdi Requiem in Berlin, Tel Aviv, and Buenos Aires. He made his Royal Opera House, Covent Garden début in 2000 as Alfredo in *La traviata*, returning in the title role of *Dom Sébastien* in 2005 and as Nemorino in *L'elisir d'amore*. He is a frequent guest at La Scala, where in addition to *Moïse et Pharaon* he has performed in *Rigoletto* and *Lucia di Lammermoor*, and he also has sung with the Teatro dell'Opera di Roma in in the Italian capital.

In 2005 he made his American début at the Metropolitan Opera in New York as Edgardo in *Lucia di Lammermoor*, receiving rave reviews. At the Met he has also sang the role of the Duke in *Rigoletto*, Nemorino in *L'elisir d'amore*, and Ruggero in *La rondine*. In the United States, in addition to the Met, he has appeared at the San Francisco Opera as Edgardo in *Lucia* and at Carnegie Hall with the Opera Orchestra of New York as Federico in *L'arlesiana*. Nemorino was the role of his debut at the Los Angeles Opera in 2009 and at the Lyric Opera of Chicago in 2010.

Giuseppe Filianoti has also performed in the major opera houses of Europe, including the Deutsche Oper Berlin, Vienna State Opera, Hamburg State Opera, and Madrid's Teatro Real, as well as leading houses in Barcelona and Florence. In recent times he has starred in a new production of *L'elisir d'amore* with the Munich State Opera and has starred as the title role in *Les contes d'Hoffmann* with the Opéra National de Paris.

### Awards
In January 1999 Giuseppe Filianoti was the winner of both the First Prize and the Top Tenor prize in the Francisco Viñas Opera Competition, and later that same year he was the second prize winner in Operalia, The World Opera Competition. In 2004, he was awarded the Franco Abbiati Italian Critics' Prize as Best Singer of the Year. In 2010, he was awarded the San Giorgio d'Oro honor by his hometown of Reggio Calabria, given annually to those from the area who have brought prestige to their hometown.
Source (edited): "http://en.wikipedia.org/wiki/Giuseppe_Filianoti"

# Inva Mula

**Inva Mula** (born 1963) is an Albanian opera soprano. She comes from an artistic family. She began her soprano career at a very early age. Her father, Avni Mula, is a famous Albanian singer and composer, born in Gjakova, a city in Kosovo. Her first name, Inva, is formed from taking her father's name, Avni, and reading it backwards.

### Life and Career
Inva was born in Tirana, Albania in 1963. In 1987 she won the *Cantante d'Albania* competition in Tirana and in 1988 the George Enescu Competition in Bucharest. In 1992 she won the *Butterfly* Competition in Barcelona. She received an award at Plácido Domingo's first *Operalia International Opera Competition* contest in Paris, 1993. A CD of the event was released.

She later performed in various concerts with the famous tenor at the Opéra Bastille in Paris, and in Brussels for Europalia Mexico, in Munich, and in Oslo. In 1996 she performed Luigi Cherubini's opera *Médée* (which was taped for TV) at Compiègne in France. She then returned for Georges Bizet's opera *La Jolie fille de Perth* (released CD, filmed for TV, and released DVD in Japan) in 1998. After this she recorded Puccini's *La Rondine* with Angela Gheorghiu for EMI and for 2005's stage production she took Gheorghiu's place in the leading role of Magda during performances in Toulouse and Paris. In 1997 she performed in a movie called The Fifth Element, where she played as Diva Plavalaguna (singing voice). Later on, she performed Bizet's *Ivan IV* concert version, which had its recital debut at Salle Pleyel in Paris, and a live recording was released as CD. In 2001, she was busy in Italy, performing Verdi's *Falstaff* at the Teatro alla Scala and *Rigoletto* at the Verona Arena, both of which were taped for TV then released on DVD.

Mula is a regular performer at La Scala, where she has sung in *Lucia di Lammermoor*, *La bohème*, and *Manon*, among others. She is also a renowned Violetta in *La Traviata*, and has sung the role in many cities around the world, including Tokyo, Bilbao, Orange, Trieste, and Toronto. In 2007, she performed Adina in *L'elisir d'amore* at Toulouse.

Her ex-husband Pirro Çako is a well-known singer and composer from Albania, so she used the spelling Tchako rather than Çako. However, after mid-1990 she began using the name Inva Mula, and never returned to the old one.

## Brief incursion in the film industry

Mula is perhaps best-known to Western filmgoers as the voice behind the Diva Plavalaguna (the very tall, blue alien performer) in the film *The Fifth Element*, where she is credited as Inva Mulla Tchako. In the film (released in 1997) she performed the aria "Oh, giusto cielo!...Il dolce suono" (the mad scene) from Gaetano Donizetti's *Lucia di Lammermoor*, and "The Diva dance" song.

Director Luc Besson adored Maria Callas, but her 1950s EMI Classics recording of "Lucia" wasn't clear enough to use on a film soundtrack, so Callas's agent Michel Glotz, who had produced this recording, introduced him to Mula.

Source (edited): "http://en.wikipedia.org/wiki/Inva_Mula"

# Isabel Bayrakdarian

**Isabel Bayrakdarian** (born 1974 in Zahlé, Lebanon) is a Grammy Award-nominated Armenian Canadian opera singer.

## Early life

Born in Lebanon in 1974, she moved to Canada as a teenager. Bayrakdarian graduated in 1997 from the University of Toronto with an honours B.A.Sc. in Engineering Science.

## Career

Isabel Bayrakdarian is noted as much for her stage presence as for her musicality, and she has followed a unique career path. Since winning first prize at the 2000 Operalia International Opera Competition founded by Plácido Domingo, she has launched an international opera career, appearing at the Metropolitan Opera, Royal Opera House, La Scala, Opéra National de Paris, Lyric Opera of Chicago, Salzburg Festival, Dresden Semperoper, Bavarian State Opera, San Francisco Opera, Santa Fe Opera, and the Canadian Opera Company among others.

Her roles have included Euridice in *Orfeo ed Euridice*, Cleopatra in *Giulio Cesare*, Romilda in *Serse*, Emilia in *Flavio*, Susanna in *The Marriage of Figaro*, Zerlina in *Don Giovanni*, Pamina in *The Magic Flute*, Rosina in *The Barber of Seville*, Marzelline in *Fidelio*, Adina in *L'elisir d'amore*, Norina in *Don Pasquale*, Leila in Bizet's *The Pearl Fishers*, Teresa in *Benvenuto Cellini*, Mélisande in *Pelléas et Mélisande*, the Vixen in *The Cunning Little Vixen*, Blanche in *Dialogues of the Carmelites* and Catherine in *A View from the Bridge*.

Her concert schedule includes appearances with the Chicago, Montreal, Toronto, Pittsburgh, and San Francisco symphony orchestras, Los Angeles Philharmonic at the Hollywood Bowl, and the National Arts Centre Orchestra, singing under the baton of such conductors as Seiji Ozawa, James Conlon, David Zinman, Michael Tilson Thomas, Christoph von Dohnányi, Christoph Eschenbach, Colin Davis, Andrew Davis, Nikolaus Harnoncourt, Mariss Jansons, Leonard Slatkin, James Levine, Peter Oundjian and Richard Bradshaw.

Bayrakdarian is the subject of a film entitled *A Long Journey Home* that documents her first trip to Armenia. A major North American tour by Bayrakdarian in October 2008 will feature the music of Reverend Gomidas (Komitas Vardapet), with concerts in Toronto, San Francisco, Orange County, Los Angeles, Vancouver, Boston and New York's Carnegie Hall. She will be accompanied by the Manitoba Chamber Orchestra conducted by Anne Manson, and pianist Serouj Kradjian. The "Remembrance Tour" is dedicated to victims of all genocides and will be sponsored by the International Institute for Genocide and Human Rights Studies (a division of Zoryan Institute).

## Prizes

In addition to her first prize at the Operalia Competition and four consecutive Juno Awards, Bayrakdarian has been awarded the Queen Elizabeth II Golden Jubilee Medal, the 2005 Virginia Parker Prize from the Canada Council for the Arts, the Leonie Rysanek Award from the George London Foundation, and a Metropolitan Opera National Council Award in 1997.

## Personal life

In 2004 she married pianist Serouj Kradjian.

## Recordings

Her first recording, titled *Joyous Light* was released in March 2002 and rose to

No. 1 in the Canadian classical charts. Soon afterwards, her vocals were featured in Atom Egoyan's film *Ararat*, and in the movie *The Lord of the Rings: The Two Towers* in the track "Evenstar".

Since then she has won four consecutive Juno Awards for "Classical Album of the Year - Vocal or Choral Performance" for the following recordings: *Azulão* (Bluebird), an album featuring Spanish and Latin American songs (2004); *Cleopatra*, featuring arias sung by the character Cleopatra from operas by Handel, Carl Heinrich Graun, Johann Adolph Hasse and Johann Mattheson (2005); *Pauline Viardot: Lieder Chansons Canzoni Mazurkas*, (2006); and *Mozart: Arie e Duetti* with fellow Canadians Russell Braun and Michael Schade (2007). In late 2007, *Tango Notturno*, a collection of tango songs, was released on CBC Records. Her album *Isabel Bayrakdarian: Gomidas Songs*, featuring songs by the 19th century Armenian composer Gomidas Vardabet, was released on September 23, 2008 on the Nonesuch label and is nominated for a Grammy in the Best Classical Vocal Performance category.

Her dance music single "Angelicus" with the Vancouver electronica group Delerium made it to the top of *Billboard* Dance music charts in March 2007 and was nominated for a Grammy Award.

### Popular and crossover

- *Millennium Gala* (2001, CBC Records)
- *Joyous Light* (2002, CBC Records)
- *The Lord of the Rings: The Two Towers* soundtrack (2002)
- *Ararat* soundtrack (2002)
- *Delerium: Nuages du Monde* (2006, Nettwerk)
- *Tango Notturno* (2007, CBC Records)
- *Gomidas Songs* (2008, Nonesuch) with Chamber Players of the Armenian Philharmonic conducted by Eduard Topchjan; Serouj Kradjian, piano

### Classical

- *Azulão* (2003, CBC Records)
- *Mahler: Symphony No. 2* (2004, San Francisco Symphony label) with Lorraine Hunt Lieberson and the San Francisco Symphony & Chorus conducted by Michael Tilson Thomas.
- *Cleopatra* (2004, CBC Records) with Tafelmusik Baroque Orchestra.
- *Pauline Viardot: Lieder Chansons Canzoni Mazurkas* (Analekta, 2004)
- *Mozart: Arie e Duetti* (2006, CBC Records) with Russell Braun, Michael Schade and the Canadian Opera Company Orchestra, conducted by Richard Bradshaw.
- *Gomidas Songs*, (2008, Nonesuch Records)

### Filmography

- *Opera Night at Cologne* (2005)
- Handel: *Serse* (2005)
- *A Long Journey Home* (2005)
- Mozart: *Don Giovanni*. Live from Salzburg (2006)
- Great Performances at the Met: *The Magic Flute* (2007)
- *Opera Under the Stars*. Live in Ottawa at LeBreton Flats Park with the Canadian Opera Company (2007)

Source (edited): "http://en.wikipedia.org/wiki/Isabel_Bayrakdarian"

# Joseph Calleja

**Joseph Calleja**, (born 22 January 1978), is a Maltese tenor. He began singing at the age of 16 and, having been discovered by Paul Asciak, continued his studies with him. At 19, he made his operatic debut as Macduff in Verdi's *Macbeth* at Astra Theatre in Gozo and went on to become a prize winner at the Belvedere Hans Gabor competition the same year. In 1998 he won the Caruso Competition in Milan and was a prize winner in Plácido Domingo's Operalia International Opera Competition in 1999. He has since been considered one of the most promising young tenors of the 21st century.

In Europe Calleja has performed in many Opera Houses including Royal Opera House in Covent Garden in London, the Vienna Staatsoper, Frankfurt Opera, Deutsche Oper Berlin, Opéra National du Rhin in Strasbourg, Teatre Principal in Majorca, Gran Teatre de Liceu in Barcelona and many more.

In the USA Calleja has performed at the Metropolitan Opera in New York, Los Angeles Opera, Seattle Opera, Washington National Opera, and the Civic Opera House in Chicago. Calleja has recorded two CDs of opera arias: *Tenor Arias* and *The Golden Voice*.

### Repertory

- Zephoris in *Si j'étais roi* (by Adolphe Adam)
- Tebaldo in *I Capuleti e i Montecchi* (by Vincenzo Bellini)
- Arturo in *I puritani* (Bellini)
- Elvino in *La sonnambula* (Bellini)
- Lind in *Isabella* (by Azio Corghi)
- Nemorino in *L'elisir d'amore* (by Gaetano Donizetti)
- Edgardo in *Lucia di Lammermoor* (Donizetti)
- Leicester in *Maria Stuarda* (Donizetti)
- Ernesto in *Don Pasquale* (Donizetti)
- Roberto Devereux in *Roberto Devereux* (Donizetti)
- Faust in *Faust* (by Charles Gounod)
- Roméo in *Roméo et Juliette* (Gounod)
- Don Ottavio in *Don Giovanni* (by Mozart)
- Rodolfo in *La bohème* (by Giacomo Puccini)
- Rinuccio in *Gianni Schicchi* (Puccini)
- Count Almaviva in *Il barbiere di Siviglia* (by Gioacchino Rossini)
- Fenton in *Falstaff* (by Giuseppe Verdi)
- Edoardo di Sanval in *Un giorno di regno* (Verdi)
- Macduff in *Macbeth* (Verdi)
- The Duke in *Rigoletto* (Verdi)
- Alfredo in *La traviata* (Verdi)
- Hoffmann in *Les contes d'Hoffmann* (Offenbach)

**Recordings and videos**

- 2003: DVD of *Maria Stuarda* featuring Calleja as Leicester, recorded by the Fondazione Orchestra Stabile de Bergamo.
- 2004: Solo recital disc, "Tenor Arias", conducted by Riccardo Chailly with the Orchestra Sinfonica e Coro di Milano.
- 2005: Solo recital disc, "The Golden Voice", conducted by Carlo Rizzi with the Academy of St. Martin in the Fields.
- Date unknown: "Puccini Discoveries"

Calleja made a guest appearance on Renée Fleming's album *By Request*, singing the role of Alfredo in the Act 1 closing scene of *La traviata*. On 19 July 2009 he sang with Michael Bolton.
Source (edited): "http://en.wikipedia.org/wiki/Joseph_Calleja"

# Joseph Kaiser

**Joseph Kaiser** is a Canadian operatic tenor. In 2005 he won 2nd prize in Placido Domingo's Operalia International Opera Competition. He has performed as a soloist with the New York Metropolitan Opera, making his debut in 2007.

In 2006, he played the role of Tamino in Kenneth Branagh's English-language film version of *The Magic Flute*. The film has been released in Europe, but not in the U.S.

Kaiser was also an anthem singer at the Bell Centre in Montreal.
Source (edited): "http://en.wikipedia.org/wiki/Joseph_Kaiser"

# José Cura

**José Cura** (born December 5, 1962) is a prominent operatic tenor known for his intense and original interpretations of his characters, notably Verdi's Otello and Saint-Saëns' Samson, as well as for his unconventional and innovative concert performances. He is also able to perform high baritone roles with the extended lower parts of his vocal range.

José Cura was born in Rosario, Argentina. He originally trained as an orchestral conductor, his vocal talents largely unrecognised until 1988 He became the first artist to sing and conduct simultaneously (both in concert and on recordings) and the first to combine singing with symphonic works in a 'half and half' concert format. Cura made operatic history when he first conducted *Cavalleria Rusticana* and then stepped on stage after intermission to sing Canio in *I Pagliacci* at the Hamburg Opera in February 2003.

A compelling actor and charismatic stage performer, Cura has been featured in numerous telecasts of opera and concert productions from venues around the world.

He created Cuibar Productions, formed by the following branches: Cuibar Phono Video (Recording Label), CuibArt (Artist Management).

He is also the Patron of the New Devon Opera and the Vice-President of British Youth Opera (BYO). In 2007 José Cura was appointed a visiting professor of the Royal Academy of Music in London.

**Career milestones**

- 1993 - Signorina Julia by Bibalo, Teatro Verdi, Trieste, Italy; first starring role
- 1994 - Le Villi by Puccini, Festival della Valle d'Itria, Italy; first recorded performance
- 1995 - Stiffelio by Verdi, R.O.H. Covent Garden, London, UK; house debut
- 1995 - Nabucco by Verdi, L'Opera National de Paris (Bastille), Paris, France; house debut
- 1996 - Samson et Dalila, R.O.H. Covent Garden, London, UK, role debut
- 1996 - Cavalleria Rusticana by Mascagni, Ravenna, Italy; first televised performance
- 1996 - Tosca by Puccini, Vienna State Opera, Vienna, Austria; house debut
- 1997 - La Gioconda by Ponchielli, Teatro alla Scala, Milan, Italy; house debut
- 1997 - Otello by Verdi, Teatro Regio, Turin, Italy; role debut, broadcast live
- 1998 - Aida by Verdi, New Imperial Theatre, Tokyo, Japan; role and house debut. Inaugural season of the new theatre and first time an opera production was fully built in Japan
- 1998 - Manon Lescaut by Puccini, Teatro alla Scala, Milan, Italy; recorded on video
- 1998 - Samson et Dalila, Washington Opera, USA, house debut
- 1999 - Cavalleria Rusticana by Mascagni, Metropolitan Opera, New York, USA; only the second tenor in Met's history to make his debut on the season's Opening Night (the other one having been Caruso in 1902)
- 2000 - La Traviata à Paris, filmed on location in Paris, France, and broadcast live to an audience of millions around the world
- 2001 - A Passion for Verdi, L.S.O., Barbican Centre, London, UK; available in DVD
- 2001 - Appointed Principal Guest Conductor of the Polish orchestra Sinfonia Varsovia
- 2002 - Created Cuibar Phono Video (CPV), the recording label of Cuibar Productions, Cura's own company. The same year, CPV releases Rachmaninov's 2° Symphony with Sinfonia Varsovia; Cura's first symphonic studio recording is considered by many to be among the

- best recordings ever of this work
- 2008 - Edgar by Puccini, Teatro Regio, Turin, Italy; first modern performance of the original version in 4 acts

**Prizes and awards**
- 1994 - 1st Prize - Plácido Domingo's Operalia International Opera Competition
- 1997 - Abbiati Award – Italian Critics Prize
- 1998 - Orphée d'Or - Académie du Disque Lyrique, France
- 1999 - Professor Honoris Causae – Universidad C.A.E.C.E, Argentina
- 1999 - Citizen of Honour – City of Rosario, Argentina
- 1999 - ECHO – Deutscher Schallplattenpreis: Sänger des Jahres, Germany
- 2000 - Chevalier de l'Ordre du Cedre - Lebanese government
- 2001 - Best Artist of the Year, Grup de Liceistes – Barcelona
- 2002 - The Ewa Czeszejko – Sochacka Foundation Award, Poland
- 2003 - Artist of the Year – Catullus Prize, Italy
- 2004 - Citizen of Honour – City of Veszprem, Hungary

Source (edited): "http://en.wikipedia.org/wiki/Jos%C3%A9_Cura"

# Joyce DiDonato

**Joyce DiDonato** (born February 13, 1969) is an award winning American operatic mezzo-soprano particularly admired for her interpretations of the works of Handel, Mozart, and Rossini. DiDonato has performed with many of the world's leading opera companies and orchestras.

## Early life and education

Joyce DiDonato was born Joyce Flaherty in Prairie Village, Kansas in 1969, the sixth of seven children in a close-knit Irish-American family. She sang in choir and musicals in high school and dreamed of becoming a Broadway star or pop singer. DiDonato entered Wichita State University (WSU) in the autumn of 1988 where she studied vocal music education. She was initially more interested in teaching high school vocal music and musical theatre and did not become interested in opera until her junior year, when she was cast in a school production of *Die Fledermaus*. After graduating from WSU in the spring of 1992, DiDonato decided to pursue graduate studies in vocal performance at the Academy of Vocal Arts. Following her studies in Philadelphia, she was accepted in Santa Fe Opera's young artist program in 1995. While there she appeared in several minor roles and understudied for larger parts in such operas as Mozart's *Le nozze di Figaro*, Richard Strauss' *Salome*, Kálmán's *Gräfin Mariza* and the 1994 world premiere of David Lang's *Modern Painters*. DiDonato was honored as the Outstanding Apprentice Artist by the Santa Fe Opera that year. In 1996 she became a part of Houston Grand Opera's young artist program where she sang from the autumn of 1996 to the spring of 1998. During the summer of 1997, DiDonato participated in San Francisco Opera's Merola Program.

During her apprentice years, DiDonato competed in several notable vocal competitions. In 1996 she won second prize in the Eleanor McCollum Competition and was a district winner of the Metropolitan Opera National Council Auditions. In 1997 she won a William Matheus Sullivan Award. In 1998 she won second prize in the Operalia Competition, first place in the Stewart Awards, won the George London Competition]], and a received a Richard F. Gold Career Grant from the Shoshana Foundation.

## Career

DiDonato began her professional career in the 1998–1999 season singing with several regional opera companies in the United States. She most notably appeared as the main heroine, Maslova, in the world premiere of Tod Machover's *Resurrection* with the Houston Grand Opera. She gave a recital in San Francisco that year as part of the Schwabacher recital series.

In the 1999–2000 season, DiDonato performed the role of Meg in the world premiere of Mark Adamo's *Little Women* at Houston Grand Opera with Stephanie Novacek as Jo and Chad Shelton as Laurie. She performed the role of Cherubino in Mozart's *Le nozze di Figaro* with Santa Fe Opera and the role of Isabella in Rossini's *L'italiana in Algeri* with the New Israeli Opera. In addition, DiDonato gave a recital at New York's Morgan Library under the auspices of the George London Foundation and sang the mezzo-soprano solos in the Seattle Symphony's production of Handel's *Messiah*.

In the 2000–2001 season, DiDonato made her debut at La Scala as Angelina in Rossini's *La Cenerentola*, returned to Houston Grand Opera as Dorabella in Mozart's *Così fan tutte*, and sang the mezzo-soprano solos in Bach's *Mass in B minor* with the Ensemble Orchestral de Paris and conductor John Nelson. In 2000, DiDonato received the ARIA (Awards Recognizing Individual Artistry) award, which annually recognized American "vocal artists of exceptional ability and undeniable promise".

In the 2001–2002 season DiDonato made her debut with Washington National Opera as Dorabella in Mozart's *Così fan tutte*, her debut with De Nederlandse Opera as Sesto in Handel's *Giulio Cesare*, her debut with Opéra National de Paris as Rosina in Rossini's *Il barbiere di Siviglia*, her debut with Bavarian State Opera as Cherubino in Mozart's *Le nozze di Figaro* under the baton of Zubin Mehta, and returned to Santa Fe Opera to perform the role of Annio in Mozart's *La clemenza di Tito*. She made several concert appearances including performances of Vivaldi's *Gloria* with Riccardo Muti and the La Scala Orchestra and Mendelssohn's *A Midsummer Night's Dream* with

Ensemble Orchestral de Paris. In 2002, DiDonato was given the Richard Tucker Award.

In the 2002–2003 season, DiDonato made her debut with the New York City Opera as Sister Helen in Jake Heggie's *Dead Man Walking*, her debut with Théâtre du Châtelet in the title role of Rossini's *La cenerentola*, her debut at Covent Garden as Zlatohrbitek the fox in Janáček's *The Cunning Little Vixen* under the baton of Sir John Eliot Gardiner, and her debut with the New National Theatre Tokyo as Rosina in Rossini's *Il barbiere di Siviglia*. She performed the title role in Rossini's *Adina* at the Rossini Opera Festival in Pesaro and the role of Cherubino in Mozart's *Le nozze di Figaro* with Opéra Bastille. In concert, DiDonato performed Mozart's *Requiem* with the Seattle Symphony, Berlioz's *Les nuits d'été* with the Ensemble Orchestral de Paris, and made her Carnegie Hall debut in a production of Bach's *Mass in B Minor* with the Orchestra of St. Luke's under the baton of Peter Schreier. She toured Europe with Marc Minkowski and Les Musiciens du Louvre in performances of *Les nuits d'été*. In 2003 DiDonato was the recipient of New York City Opera's Richard Gold Debut Award

In the 2003–2004 season, DiDonato made her debut with the San Francisco Opera as Rosina in Rossini's *Il barbiere di Siviglia* and reprised the role with Houston Grand Opera. She performed Idamante in Mozart's *Idomeneo* with De Nederlandse Opera and at the Aix-en-Provence Festival. She sang the role of Ascanio in a concert performance of Berlioz's *Benvenuto Cellini* with the Orchestre National de France and appeared in solo recitals at the Lincoln Center, the Kennedy Center, Kansas City's Folly Theater, and Wigmore Hall among others. She sang at the Hollywood Bowl in a production of Beethoven's *Symphony No. 9* with the Los Angeles Philharmonic.

In the 2004–2005 season, DiDonato made her debut with the Grand Théâtre de Genève as Elisabetta in Donizetti's *Maria Stuarda*. She returned to La Scala in the role of Angelina in Rossini's *La Cenerentola* and once again played Rosina in a new production of Rossini's *Il barbiere di Siviglia* by Luca Ronconi at the Pesaro Festival and the Teatro Comunale di Bologna.

In the 2005–2006 season, DiDonato made her Metropolitan Opera debut as Cherubino in *Le nozze di Figaro* and played Stéphano in Gounod's *Roméo et Juliette* at the Met. She returned to the Royal Opera House as Rosina in *Il barbiere di Siviglia*, sang her first Sesto in Mozart's *La clemenza di Tito* with Grand Théâtre de Genève, and sang the role of Dejanira in Handel's *Hercules* at the Brooklyn Academy of Music in New York and at the Barbican Centre in London with William Christie (musician). In addition, DiDonato appeared in several concerts with the New York Philharmonic and gave a recital at Wigmore Hall in London. She closed the Santa Fe Opera's 50th anniversary season in the title role of Massenet's *Cendrillon*. In 2006, DiDonato was given the Royal Philharmonic Society Singer Award.

In the 2006–2007 season, DiDonato debuted at the Teatro Real as the Composer in Richard Strauss' *Ariadne auf Naxos*, returned to the Opéra National de Paris as Idamante in Mozart's *Idomeneo*, and returned to Houston Grand Opera as Angelina in *La Cenerentola*. She sang Rosina in *Il barbiere di Siviglia* at the Metropolitan Opera and sang her first Octavian in Richard Strauss' *Der Rosenkavalier* with the San Francisco Opera. She toured the U.S. and Europe on an extensive recital tour with accompianist Julius Drake. DiDonato won the Metropolitan Opera's Beverly Sills Award in 2007.

In the 2007–2008 season, DiDonato debuted at the Liceu as Angelina in *La Cenerentola* and at the Lyric Opera of Chicago as Rosina in *Il barbiere di Siviglia*. She sang the title role in Handel's *Alcina* with Alan Curtis and Il Complesso Barocco and the title role in Handel's *Ariodante* at the Grand Théâtre de Genève. She sang Roméo in Bellini's *I Capuleti e i Montecchi* with Opéra Bastille and returned to Madrid's Teatro Real as Idamante in *Idomeneo* in July 2008. DiDonato also gave recitals at La Scala, Lincoln Center, and the Brooklyn Academy of Music, and performed a special concert of Handel arias which was recorded in Brussels.

In the 2008–2009 season, DiDonato returned to Covent Garden as Donna Elvira in Mozart's *Don Giovanni* and as Rosina in *Il barbiere di Siviglia*. In a performance of that opera on July 7, DiDonato slipped onstage and broke her right fibula; she finished the first act hobbling and the rest of the performance on crutches. She then performed the five remaining scheduled performances from a wheelchair. She will be performing the roles of Beatrice in Berlioz's *Béatrice et Bénédict* with Houston Grand Opera, Idamante in Mozart's *Idomeneo* with Opéra National de Paris, and Rosina in *Il barbiere di Siviglia* in her debut with Vienna State Opera. DiDonato will appear in concerts with the New York Philharmonic, Kansas City Symphony, and the Metropolitan Opera Orchestra, the latter of which under the baton of James Levine. She will be touring Europe and the United States with Les Talens Lyriques giving concerts of Handel arias and will give performances at Wigmore Hall and the Rossini Opera Festival.

In October 2010, DiDonated won the Klassik Echo Award as Singer of the Year.

DiDonato has sung in concert with the SWR Orchestra Kaiserslautern, The King's Consort, the Orchestra of the Eighteenth Century, the Cleveland Orchestra, and the San Francisco Symphony.

### Personal life

DiDonato is married to Italian conductor Leonardo Vordoni with whom she lives in Kansas City, Missouri. She was married once previously and continues to use her first husband's surname professionally.

@ Indicates a world premiere

### Listen

- Rosina on YouTube in Rossini's *The Barber of Seville*
- Angelina (Cenerentola) on YouTube in Rossini's *La Cenerentola*

- Elmira on YouTube in Handel's *Floridante*
- Donna Elvira on YouTube in Mozart's *Don Giovanni*

### Discography

**Complete opera recordings**

- Alcina in Handel's *Alcina* with conductor Alan Curtis and Il Complesso Barocco, released 2009, Archiv label.
- Angelina (Cenerentola) in Rossini's *La Cenerentola* with conductor Alberto Zedda and SWR Orchestra Kaiserslautern, released 2005, Naxos label.
- Ascanio in Berlioz's *Benvenuto Cellini* with conductor John Nelson and Orchestre National de France, released 2005, Virgin Classics label.
- Elmira in Handel's *Floridante* with conductor Alan Curtis and Il Complesso Barocco, released 2007, Archiv Produktion label.
- Grace Kelly in Michael Daugherty's *Jackie O* with conductor Christopher Larkin and Houston Grand Opera Orchestra, released 1997, Argo label.
- Maslova in Tod Machover's *Resurrection* with conductor Patrick Summers and Houston Grand Opera Orchestra, released 1999, Albany Records.
- Meg March in Mark Adamo's *Little Women* with conductor Katherine Ciesinski and Houston Grand Opera Orchestra, released 2001, Ondine label.
- Radamisto in Handel's *Radamisto* with conductor Alan Curtis and Il Complesso Barocco, released 2005, Virgin Classics label.

**Concert recordings**

- *Antonio Vivaldi: The Complete Sacred Music* with conductor Robert King and The King's Consort, released 2005, Hyperion label.
- *Mendelssohn: A Midsummer Nights Dream* with conductor John Nelson and the Ensemble Orchestral de Paris, released 2003, EMI Classics label.
- *Mozart: The Last Concerto 1791* with conductor Frans Brüggen and the Orchestra of the Eighteenth Century, released 2002, Glossa label.

**Solo recordings**

- *Rossini: Colbran, the Muse*, conductor Edoardo Muller and Orchestra dell'Accademia Nazionale di Santa Cecilia, released 2009, Virgin Classics label.
- *Furore – Mad Scenes from Operas*, conductor Christophe Rousset and Les Talens Lyriques, released 2008, Virgin Classics label.
- *Amor e gelosia: Handel Operatic Duets* with Patrizia Ciofi, conductor Alan Curtis and Il Complesso Barocco, released 2004, Virgin Classics label.
- *The Deepest Desire*, accompanied by David Zobel, released 2006, Eloquentia label.
- *Joyce DiDonato: Songs by Fauré, Hahn and Head · Arias by Rossini and Handel*, live recording at Wigmore Hall, accompanied by Julius Drake, released 2006, Wigmore Hall Live label.
- *¡Pasión!*, accompanied by Julius Drake, released 2007, Eloquentia label.
- *Diva, Divo*, with the Orchestre et Choeur de l'Opera National de Lyon under Kazushi Ono, released 2011

**Other recordings**

- *William Barnewitz: Long Road Home*, DiDonato appears as a guest artist, released 2007, Avie label.
- *Plácido Domingo's Operalia '98: A Tribute to Passion and Soul*, released 1998, Montblanc label.

**Film and television appearances**

- Meg March in Mark Adamo's *Little Women* with conductor Katherine Ciesinski and Houston Grand Opera Orchestra, aired on PBS' *Great Performances* in 2001.
- Rosina in Rossini's *Il barbiere di Siviglia* with conductor Bruno Campanella and Opéra National de Paris, aired on television in 2002, released on DVD 2002.
- "Gala Jean-Philippe Rameau" – Concert du 20ème anniversaire des Musiciens du Louvre, aired on television in 2003.
- Dejanira in Handel's *Hercules* with conductor William Christie, Les Arts Florissants, and Aix-en-Provence Festival, aired on television in 2005, released on DVD 2005.
- Rosina in Rossini's *Il barbiere di Siviglia* with conductor Antonio Pappano at the Royal Opera House, released on DVD in 2010
- Angelina in Rossini's *La Cenerentola* with conductor Patrick Summers at the Gran Teatre del Liceu, released on DVD in 2010

Source (edited): "http://en.wikipedia.org/wiki/Joyce_DiDonato"

# Kate Aldrich

**Kate Aldrich** (b. October 31, 1973, Damariscotta, Maine) is an American mezzo soprano.

She has performed with the Metropolitan Opera, San Francisco Opera, Teatro Colón in Buenos Aires, the Hamburg State Opera, Teatro Regio of Torino, Los Angeles Opera, L'Opéra de Montréal, the Deutsche Oper am Rhein in Düsseldorf, Teatro Nacional de São Carlos in Lisbon, National Theatre in Prague, and the New York City Opera.

Her roles include Carmen, Antoine Mariotte's Salome, Octavian in *Der Rosenkavalier*, Cesare and Sesto in *Giulio Cesare*, Isabella in *L'italiana in Algeri*, Rosina in *Il barbiere di Siviglia*, Angelina in *La Cenerentola*, Arsace in *Semiramide*, Fenena in *Nabucco*, Preziosilla in *La forza del destino*, Eboli in *Don Carlos*, Dalila in *Samson et Dalila*, Sesto in *La clemenza di Tito*, and Dulcinée in *Don Quichotte*.

Aldrich rose to international fame in

2002 through her starring role in the Zeffirelli production of *Aida*. That same year she won the CulturArte Award at the Operalia International Opera Competition, in 2006 she won the Alfréd Radok Award and the Thalia Award in the Czech Republic.

### Filmography
- Verdi, *Aida* (Zeffirelli, 2002)
- *Roberto Alagna and Friends* (2005)

Source (edited): "http://en.wikipedia.org/wiki/Kate_Aldrich"

## Lisette Oropesa

**Lisette Oropesa** (born on September 29, 1983, in New Orleans) is an American soprano, who was raised in Baton Rouge, where she studied at Louisiana State University. Her parents are both emigrants from Cuba, and her mother, Rebeca Oropesa (née Ulloa), is a soprano who was heard in productions at Loyola University of the South (Sister Genevieve in *Suor Angelica*, and Venus in *Venus and Adonis*) and LSU (Lauretta in *Gianni Schicchi*), before she decided on raising a family.

Lisette Oropesa was in the National Council Grand Finals Concert, at the Metropolitan Opera, in 2005, and was then part of the Lindemann Young Artists Development Program until 2008. She made her Met debut in a small role in Jean-Pierre Ponnelle's production of *Idomeneo* (conducted by James Levine), on September 28, 2006, then sang the First Lay-Sister in their new production of *Suor Angelica*.

As substitute, she sang her first leading role at that house, Susanna in Sir Jonathan Miller's production of *Le nozze di Figaro* (opposite Erwin Schrott's Figaro), on October 2, 2007, which was reckoned a great success.

In the 2007-08 season, Miss Oropesa was seen in the Met's *Hänsel und Gretel*, as the Dew Fairy, and, in the 2008-09 season, as the role of Lisette in *La rondine*, opposite Angela Gheorghiu, Roberto Alagna, and Samuel Ramey, in Nicolas Joël's production. She also sang the role of the Rhinemaiden, Woglinde, in the Met's 2009 *Der Ring des Nibelungen*, and additionally sang the off-stage role of the Woodbird in *Siegfried*. On September 27, 2010, she reprised her Rhinemaiden in the Met's season-opening production of *Das Rheingold*.

Elsewhere, the soprano has appeared with the Welsh National Opera (Constanze in *Die Entführung aus dem Serail*), Deutsche Oper am Rhein (*Il turco in Italia*), Tanglewood Music Festival (Constanze), Ravinia Festival (*Le nozze di Figaro*, conducted by James Conlon), Opera New Jersey (*Lucia di Lammermoor*), Arizona Opera (Gilda in *Rigoletto*), and the New Orleans Opera Association (*Rigoletto* and *Les pêcheurs de perles*).

### Videography
- Humperdinck: *Hänsel und Gretel* (Shäfer, Coote; Jurowsky, Jones, 2008) EMI
- Puccini: *La rondine* (Gheorghiu, Alagna, Brenciu, Ramey; Armiliato, Joël, 2009) EMI

### Awards
- Grand Finals winner, Metropolitan Opera National Council Auditions, 2005.
- Special Winner, Gerda Lissner Foundation, 2008.
- First Place award, Licia Albanese Puccini Competition.
- George London Award.
- Sarah Tucker study grant.
- Zarzuela Award, Operalia International Opera Competition, 2007.
- Sullivan Foundation Award.

Source (edited): "http://en.wikipedia.org/wiki/Lisette_Oropesa"

## Maria Fontosh

**Maria Fontosh**, born 5 June 1976 is a Ukrainian born Russian soprano residing in Sweden. She is a part of the Royal Swedish Opera's ensemble for which she made her debut as Rosina in The Barber of Seville in 2001.

### Background

Fontosh was born in Ukraine but grew up in Russia where she studied piano, singing and conducting. After moving to Sweden she conducted studies at the Falun Conservatory of Music, the Royal Swedish Academy of Music (Kungliga Musikaliska Akademien) and the University College of Opera (Operahögskolan). Fontosh graduated from the University College of Opera in Stockholm in December 2001.

In 1999 Fontosh won 4th prize in the Mirjam Helin International Singing Competition in Helsinki. In 2002 she won the 3rd prize in Plácido Domingo's Operalia International Opera Competition in Paris.

On 5 September 2007 Fontosh sang at the Värmland Classic Festival together with José Carreras, among the pieces was Franz Lehár's "The Merry Widow".

### Recent stage roles
- Lauretta, *La conversazione and I rivali delusi* (intermezzi by Niccolò Jommelli) (1999, Vadstena Academy)
- Rosina, *The Barber of Seville* (2001/2002, Royal Swedish Opera)
- Musetta, *La bohème* (2001/2002, Royal Swedish Opera)
- Zerlina, *Don Giovanni* (2002, The Ruhr Triennale)
- Fiordiligi, *Così fan tutte* (Frankfurt Opera House)
- Adina, *L'elisir d'amore* (Frankfurt Opera House)

- Zerlina, *Don Giovanni* (Frankfurt Opera House)
- Ginevra, *Ariodante* (Frankfurt Opera House)
- Marie, *The Bartered Bride* (2003/2004, Royal Swedish Opera)
- Marguerite, *Faust* (2005, Malmö Opera)
- Ginevra, *Ariodante* (2005, Frankfurt Opera House)
- Tatyana, *Eugene Onegin* (2005, Royal Swedish Opera)
- Musetta, *La bohème* (2005, Opéra National de Paris)
- Marie, *The Bartered Bride* (2006, Frankfurt Opera House)
- Marzerlline, *Fidelio* (2006, El Teatro de Ópera de Valencia)
- Countess Almaviva, *The Marriage of Figaro* (2007, Frankfurt Opera House)
- Fiordiligi, *Così fan tutte* (2007, Royal Swedish Opera)
- Violetta, *La traviata* (2007, Royal Swedish Opera)
- Antonia, *Les contes d'Hoffmann* (2008, Teatro Nacional de São Carlos)
- Marguerite, *Faust* (2008, Frankfurt Opera House)
- Mimì, La bohème, 2008, Royal Swedish Opera
- Countess Almaviva, Le nozze di Figaro, 2010 Royal Swedish Opera

**Recordings**

- *Wolfgang Amadeus Mozart: Mitridate* The Danish Radio Sinfonietta Universal 2002
- *Puccini: Discoveries* Decca 2004
- *Igor Stravinsky: Le sacre du printemps/Mavra* Budapest Music Center 2006

Source (edited): "http://en.wikipedia.org/wiki/Maria_Fontosh"

## Mikhail Petrenko

**Mikhail Petrenko** is a **Canadian Cinematographer** (DOP). Ukrainian-born Mikhail graduated from University of Indianapolis and York University with BFA in Cinematography. Mikhail currently lives in Toronto, Ontario.

**Films and Awards**

- *Morning Will Come* by Pouyan Jafarizadeh Dezfoulian —TIFF (students showcase) nominee (2008), CSC nominee for Best Student Cinematography (2009), Los Angeles International Film Festival nominee (2008), Montreal Film Festival nominee (2008)
- *Park of Lonely Benches* — Best Short Film and Audience Choice awards at Frame Film Festival (2006)
- *Patient* by Daniel T. N. Clements —Official Choice at Cannes Short Film Corner - Festival de Cannes

Source (edited): "http://en.wikipedia.org/wiki/Mikhail_Petrenko"

## Nina Stemme

Swedish soprano **Nina Stemme** (born May 11, 1963 in Stockholm) is an opera singer renowned for her warm, solid spinto soprano voice, with some qualities of a dramatic soprano.

Parallel to her studies of business administration and economics at the University of Stockholm Nina Stemme followed a 2-years-course at the Stockholm Operastudio. Her debut as Cherubino in Cortona, Italy, in 1989 made Miss Stemme decide to follow a professional singer's career; her studies at the National College of Opera in Stockholm were completed in 1994. Next to two minor roles at the Royal Swedish Opera in Stockholm she had sung in the meantime Rosalinde (*Die Fledermaus*), Mimi (*La bohème*), Euridice in Gluck's *Orfeo ed Euridice*, and Diana (*La fedeltà premiata* by Haydn).

Two internationally acclaimed singing competitions (Plácido Domingo Competition and Cardiff Singer of the World) put the soprano on the international map of promising talents. As winner of the Domingo competition the famous tenor invited her to appear with him in a concert at La Bastille (1993); the same concert also took place on January 1, 1994 in Munich.

The Swedish soprano is in great demand at the major opera houses. Since her operatic debut as Cherubino in Cortona, Italy, she has appeared with many of the greatest opera companies of the world including the Royal Swedish Opera Stockholm, the Vienna State Opera, Semperoper Dresden, Geneva, Zürich, Teatro San Carlo Naples, Gran Teatre del Liceu Barcelona, the Royal Opera House Covent Garden, the Metropolitan Opera New York, and San Francisco Opera, as well as at the Bayreuth, Salzburg, Savonlinna, Glyndebourne and Bregenz festivals.

Her roles include Rosalinde, Mimi in *La bohème*, Cio-Cio-San in *Madame Butterfly*, *Tosca*, *Manon Lescaut*, Suor Angelica, Euridice, Katerina in *Lady Macbeth of Mtsensk*, the Countess in *Le nozze di Figaro*, Marguerite, Agathe, Marie, Nyssia (König Kandaules), Jenůfa, Marschallin, Eva, Elisabeth, Elsa, Senta, Sieglinde, Elisabeth in *Tannhäuser* and Isolde. This last brought her great critical acclaim at Glyndebourne Festival Opera in 2003, on disc for EMI Classics with Plácido Domingo, Antonio Pappano and the chorus and orchestra of the Royal Opera, Covent Garden released in 2005 and most recently at the Bayreuth Festival in 2005 and again in 2006. In 2007 Nina returns with the role of Isolde to Glyndebourne Festival Opera where she first made her Debut in the role.

In 2006, Nina Stemme sang Maria in the premiere of Sven-David Sandström's Ordet - en passion, on 24 March in Stockholm. She also made her successful role debut in the title role of *Aida in a new production at Zürich Opera and recorded her first album as an exclusive artist for EMI Classics of Strauss's Four Last Songs and final scenes.

In 2008, the Swedish soprano replaced Deborah Voigt in what would have been the American soprano's role debut as Brünnhilde in the new Wiener Staatsoper Ring cycle conducted by Franz Welser-Möst. She sang the *Siegfried* Brünnhilde to great acclaim, although Eva Johansson is singing Brünnhilde for the *Götterdämmerung* being premiered next season. Stemme's official debut as Brünnhilde would have been during the 2009-2010 season at the San Francisco opera under the leadership of Donald Runnicles.

Future engagements include amongst others, *Arabella* in Gothenburg, *Ariadne auf Naxos* at Geneva Opera, Leonore (*La forza del destino*) at Vienna State Opera, Amelia (*Simon Boccanegra*) at the Royal Opera, Covent Garden, Sieglinde in the new *Ring* cycle at Vienna State Opera and in San Francisco, Salome at Geneva Opera, the Gran Teatre del Liceu Barcelona and Teatro Real Madrid, Marschallin (*Der Rosenkavalier*) at Deutsche Oper Berlin, Katerina Ismailova (*Lady Macbeth of Mtsensk*) at the Metropolitan Opera New York and her first Kundry (*Parsifal*) at the Gran Teatre del Liceu in Barcelona. On the concert platform in 2006/7 she appeared in recital with Antonio Pappano (piano) in Barcelona and Dresden, in concert performances of *Salome* in Strasbourg and Paris and in recital at the Zurich opera.

Nina Stemme is a member of the ensemble of the Royal Swedish Opera, Stockholm, where she has been named *Hovsångerska* in 2006.

Source (edited): "http://en.wikipedia.org/wiki/Nina_Stemme"

# Robert Pomakov

**Robert Pomakov** (born February 25, 1981) is a Canadian operatic bass.

Born in Toronto, Pomakov graduated from St. Michael's Choir School, Toronto, in 1999, and later studied at the Curtis Institute of Music. He performed at the LuminaTO "Luna Gala".

### Recordings

- Handel: *Apollo and Dafne/Alchemist*
- European Union Baroque Orchestra under Roy Goodman
- Naxos CD 8.555712

Source (edited): "http://en.wikipedia.org/wiki/Robert_Pomakov"

# Rolando Villazón

**Emilio Rolando Villazón Mauleón** (born February 22, 1972), is a Mexican-born tenor who settled in France and in 2007 became a French citizen.

### Early life and education

He was raised in Fuentes de Satélite, a suburban area of Greater Mexico City, Mexico. In an interview for Mexican television, Villazón told the story of how he was discovered as a tenor. He said that one day, as he was getting out of the shower in his apartment in Mexico City, somebody came knocking on his door; it was baritone Arturo Nieto, a friend of his neighbour, who had heard him singing while in the shower. He told Rolando he had an amazing voice and invited him to his music academy to develop his voice, there Rolando fell in love with opera.

### Career

#### Late 1990s and early 2000s

He came to international attention in 1999 when he won both first prizes awarded in the Operalia international competition - both for opera and zarzuela. The same year he sang for the first time in Italy as des Grieux in *Manon* at the San Felice in Genoa. In 2000 he appeared for the first time at the Berlin State Opera - as Macduff in *Macbeth*. Over the years he has presented many of his best roles there, among them José in *Carmen* and des Grieux in *Manon*.

In Munich in 2000 he sang Rodolfo in *La bohème* and in 2002 in Los Angeles, Rinuccio in *Gianni Schicchi*. In 2003 he sang Rodolfo at the Glyndebourne Festival Opera in England. He also enjoyed a huge success in the title role of *Les Contes d'Hoffmann* at Covent Garden, London. The following year he appeared, again singing the role of Alfredo in *La traviata* at the Metropolitan Opera, New York and in 2005, both at St. Petersburg and the Salzburg Festival.

In addition to his appearances on the opera stage, he has an active recording career. He has recorded four solo CDs with Virgin Classics and is additionally featured, along with Patrizia Ciofi and Topi Lehtipuu, on the recording of *Il combattimento di Tancredi e Clorinda* by Claudio Monteverdi, conducted by Emmanuelle Haïm.

#### 2005-2010

In August 2005, he sang a highly regarded Alfredo in Verdi's *La traviata* at the Salzburg Festival, conducted by Carlo Rizzi, directed by Willy Decker. Co-starring was Anna Netrebko as Violetta. They have also appeared together in a video version of Donizetti's *L'elisir d'amore*.

In 2007, Villazón switched his recording company and signed an exclusive long-term contract with Deutsche Grammophon. An album of zarzuelas (Gitano, Virgin Classics) conducted by Plácido Domingo, was released in Spring 2007. The U.S. version of his album *Viva Villazón* (Virgin Classics) was released in September 2007. In early 2010 he was a mentor and judge in the ITV show Popstar to Operastar.

#### Vocal surgery and the return to the

stage

In 2007, Villazon cancelled many of his scheduled engagements in order to diagnose and remedy a persistent vocal issue. In May 2009, Rolando Villazon announced that he had to undergo surgery in order to remove a congenital cyst in one of his vocal cords. After completing his rehabilitation, he returned to the stage in March 2010 singing Nemorino in *L'elisir d'amore* at the Vienna State Opera in March 2010, and then embarked on a series of recitals. He made his debut as a stage director with a new production of *Werther* at the Opéra de Lyon in January 2011.

### Discography

- *Romeo y Julieta* CD (2002), Radio Televisión Española
- *Der Fliegende Holländer* CD (2002), Teldec Classics
- *Berlioz: La Révolution Grecque* CD (2004), EMI Classics
- *Italian Opera Arias* CD (2004), Virgin Classics
- *Gounod & Massenet Arias* CD (2005), Virgin Classics
- *Tristan und Isolde* CDs and DVD (2005), EMI Classics
- *Don Carlo* 2 DVDs (2005), Opus Arte
- *La Traviata* CD (2005), Deutsche Grammophon
- *Merry Christmas* (Soundtrack) CD (2005), Virgin Classics
- *Opera Recital* CD; bonus edition with DVD (2006), Virgin Classics
- *La Traviata* DVD; premium 2-DVD edition (behind the scenes, rehearsals, introduction to the opera etc.) (2006), Salzburger Festspiele 2005, Deutsche Grammophon
- *La Bohème* DVD (2006), Bregenzer Festspiele 2002, ORF + Capriccio
- *Monteverdi: Il Combattimento* CD; bonus edition with DVD (2006), Virgin Classics
- *Donizetti: L'elisir d'amore* DVD (2006), Virgin Classics
- *The Berlin Concert: Live from the Waldbühne* DVD (2006), Deutsche Grammophon
- *Gitano* CD; bonus edition with DVD (February 2007), Virgin Classics
- *Duets* featuring Rolando Villazón and Anna Netrebko CD; bonus edition with DVD (March 2007), Deutsche Grammophon
- *Viva Villazón* - Rolando Villazón - Best Of CD (2007), Virgin Classics
- *La Bohème* Live recording CD (two disk set) (2008), Deutsche Grammophon
- *Romeo et Juliette"* 2 DVDs (Salzburger Festspiele 2008) (2009), Deutsche Grammophon
- *Georg Friedrich Händel"* CD/ CD+DVD,(2009) Deutsche Grammophon
- *La Bohème* DVD (2009)

Source (edited): "http://en.wikipedia.org/wiki/Rolando_Villaz%C3%B3n"

# Susanna Phillips

**Susanna Phillips** is a soprano opera singer. She has appeared at the Lyric Opera of Chicago and the Metropolitan Opera, among others. Though born in Birmingham, Alabama she and her family moved two weeks after she was born, to Huntsville, Madison County, Alabama; where she grew up and attended school at Randolph School. While attending Randolph, she also began studying voice with Ginger Beazley at Ars Nova School of the Arts. There her talents flourished and she soon found herself accepted to the Juilliard School in New York.

At Juilliard, Susanna became a student of Cynthia Hoffmann and began coursework for a Bachelor of Music degree in 1999, continuing there until receiving a Master of Music degree in 2004 followed by becoming a member of the Santa Fe Opera's Apprentice Program for Singers during the summer 2004 season, "covering" the role of "Donna Elvira".

In recent years, she has won a number of awards and prestige from her well regarded performances, including having been named a soloist for the New York Pops at Carnegie Hall, winning $15,000 at the Metropolitan Opera Council Auditions in March 2005, and most recently winning the women's division and the People's Choice awards at Plácido Domingo's Operalia International Opera Competition in Madrid for $30,000 and $10,000 respectively. In March 2005, Phillips joined Lyric Opera Center for American Artists at the Chicago Lyric Opera.

She participated in Santa Fe's "50th Anniversary Arias Gala Concert" on 12 August 2006 and sang the role of "Pamina" in the final two performances of the 2006 season production of *The Magic Flute*. For Santa Fe's 2007 season, she sang the role of Fiordiligi in *Cosi fan tutte*. She sang Pamina at the Met in 2010-2011.

Source (edited): "http://en.wikipedia.org/wiki/Susanna_Phillips"

# Thiago Arancam

Tenor Thiago Arancam

**Thiago Arancam** (born 6 February 1982, São Paulo) is an Italian-Brazilian lirico spinto tenor. He graduated from the La Scala Academy in 2007. In 2008, he won three prizes at Operalia.

## Biography and career

Thiago Arancam started his studies in São Paulo at the "Municipal School of Music" and continued at the Musical University "Carlos Gomes", where he graduated in "Erudite Chant" in 2003. He won the prestigious "Prêmio Revelação" (Revelation Prize) of the 5th Bidu Sayão International Vocal Competition in 2004.

Soon after, he was invited to attend the "Accademia delle Arti e dei Mestieri", associated with the "La Scala" in Milan, Italy. He is the first Brazilian to be taken into the Academy, directed by great soprano Leyla Gencer. It is there that he met his present voice teacher, Vincenzo Manno. He debuted in a lyric concert at "La Scala" on 27 February 2005.

In 2007, he participated in concerts with the Orchestra Sinfonica of the Friuli-Venezia Giulia, singing Zarzuela arias and classical Spanish songs. He received the critic award for the best emergent young voice 2007/2008 "Premio Alto Adige - Talento emergente della lirica 2007/2008" in Bolzano. In December 2007 he debuted in Puccini's first opera, "Le Villi", in the role of Roberto at "Teatro Coccia" of Novara and at "Teatro Sociale" of Mantua.

In 2008, he performed in the United Arab Emirates, with the orchestra of La Scala and in two concerts with the Orchestra Camerata Brasil of Brasilia, conducted by Maestro Silvio Barbato. He was chosen to participate to the famous lyric competition "Operalia 2008", where the jury awarded him three prizes: First Zarzuela Prize "Don Plácido Domingo", First Audience Prize and Second Opera Prize.

On 8 November 2008, Arancam debuted in the United States of America with the role of Don Josè in, George Bizet's *Carmen*, at Washington National Opera, with mezzo-soprano Denyce Graves, conducted by Julius Rudel.

In 2009 he played the roles of Cavaradossi in Tosca at Frankfurt Opera House, Maurizio in Adriana Lecouvreur at Teatro Regio in Turin, Radames in Aida in France, at the Sanxay Lyric Festival, and he sang a recital in London at St.John's (Rosenblatt Recitals).

## Discography

- *Arias*, 2004, TBA Records

## Awards

- "Prêmio Revelação" 5th Bidu Sayão International Vocal Competition 2004.
- "Premio Alto Adige – Talento Emergente della Lirica 2007/2008", by the lyric association "L'Obiettivo" of Bolzano, during the Operetta Festival "La musa leggera".
- "Operalia 2008" - First Zarzuela Prize "Don Placido Domingo", First Audience Prize, and Second Opera Prize.

Source (edited): "http://en.wikipedia.org/wiki/Thiago_Arancam"